G000093558

an

adventure

in

education

an
adventure
in
education

DEREK ESP

Copyright © 2019 Derek Esp

The moral right of the author has been asserted.

Apart from any fair dealing for the purposes of research or private study,
or criticism or review, as permitted under the Copyright, Designs and Patents
Act 1988, this publication may only be reproduced, stored or transmitted, in
any form or by any means, with the prior permission in writing of the
publishers, or in the case of reprographic reproduction in accordance with
the terms of licences issued by the Copyright Licensing Agency. Enquiries
concerning reproduction outside those terms should be sent to the publishers.

Matador
9 Priory Business Park,
Wistow Road, Kibworth Beauchamp,
Leicestershire. LE8 0RX
Tel: 0116 279 2299
Email: books@troubador.co.uk
Web: www.troubador.co.uk/matador
Twitter: @matadorbooks

ISBN 978 1838590 048

British Library Cataloguing in Publication Data.
A catalogue record for this book is available from the British Library.

Printed and bound in the UK by T J International, Padstow, Cornwall
Typeset in 11pt Garamond by Troubador Publishing Ltd, Leicester, UK

Matador is an imprint of Troubador Publishing Ltd

This book is dedicated to my wife Gill, my fellow adventurer for almost fifty years. As well as being described as 'a wonderful wife, mother and granny' Gill was the inspirational leader of our growing family and a caring and active initiator of developments in our lovely Somerset village. She was a constant and loving support in the highs and lows of our adventures in education.

Contents

introduction

───

This book is the result of a suggestion from the University of Exeter education department. In 2012, I had completed an MA in the history department. When I asked the education department if I could follow up my seventeenth-century historical research their response was: 'we don't do the seventeenth century'. Instead they invited me to write about my life in education. I was intrigued to think that I now qualified as a part of education history so I agreed.

Autobiography has now become fashionable as a valid source of historical evidence. Historical evidence is not value free. This is particularly the case when history is written by the winners. The 'cultural turn' in history has legitimised subjectivity to some degree and social sciences now encourage autobiography and other new approaches which are meant to stimulate debate and influence contemporary thought.

This 'adventure in education' is an opportunity to examine the influences on my learning as well as my work in education. It has been fun to explore my own experiences.

I have taken the liberty of commenting on current educational plans and preoccupations but it is not to be taken to heart. It is no surprise that we keep on reorganising ourselves. A Danish poet put it this way, 'man is an animal that draws lines and then falls over them'. This is true for us all, especially educators and politicians. Many of our decisions are ad hoc ones to address immediate crises and sometimes put expediency before good sense. One chair of education I worked with always spoke of a 'haddock' (ad hoc) solution, and such solutions are always around in politics and the busy and ever-changing world of education.

1

early years

My Shropshire home town, Bridgnorth, sits on two banks of the River Severn. It is an historical market town with some light industry. On the west bank is High Town set on a cliff above the river, containing the two parish churches of St Mary's and St Leonard's. Low Town once housed many of the workforce of the carpet factory and other manufacturing businesses. It also had several pubs and cafés serving the tourists. A funicular railway still links the High Town and Low Town. My mother was once stuck on the funicular railway when it broke down. She was the sole passenger and had to be escorted to safety by the fire service. This was big news and made the front page of the *Bridgnorth Journal*. Most of Low Town is on the left bank of the River Severn is crossed by means of our historic bridge.

The town was called 'the Venice of the North' by some visitors when it was a popular day trip for West Midland fishermen and tourists. When I was a child there was a local, possibly apocryphal, story that a town councillor proposed that our town should have a gondola on the river as an additional enhancement to the two fleets of rowing boats hired out to day trippers. Another councillor thought this was a good idea but suggested that they should buy two gondolas and breed them.

High Town has a lovely park and the leaning ruins of the castle keep which was destroyed by Cromwell's forces. This was supposedly a borough loyal to the King but, as they retreated, the garrison was pelted with vegetables by the townspeople. To make matters worse for royalists the curate at St Leonard's was Richard Baxter, a future leader of the Puritans, who refused the offer of a bishopric on the return of Charles II in 1660. Baxter had moved to Kidderminster in Cromwell's time where he built up a large independent church. He was glad to get out of Bridgnorth where he found that our 'hearts were harder than the sandstone rock of which the church was built'.

My maternal grandmother, 'Granny', had returned as a widow from New Zealand to England in 1904 with two children, my mother, Dorothy, and her brother, George. She bought a temperance hotel and sweet shop and soon married again bearing another daughter and three more sons. At the time of my birth in 1934 my parents Edward (Ted) and Dorothy rented a small cottage halfway up a very long flight of steps between High Town and Low Town. This meant that I started life in a neutral position and like the grand old Duke of York I was 'neither up nor down'.

My father was the eldest of seven children from a farming family at Easthope on the Wenlock Edge. In the 1930s times were hard for hill farmers. My father wanted to go to Argentina but my grandfather, Richard, refused to let him go so my father left the farm and travelled east to Bridgnorth where he sold seeds to farmers. That is where he met my mother, Dorothy.

After my birth, seven years into their marriage, we moved to a council house on the northern edge of High Town. Our road, The Innage, was very close to the countryside. The adjacent stream and woods offered exciting adventures for a child. I am told I was a somewhat assertive toddler. Each morning I used to visit a kind old lady dressed in black who was our neighbour. I used to knock loudly on her door and demand 'bickets'. I remember my first experience of the hard realities of life at the age of three. A six-year-old boy, Tony, was teaching me to play marbles one day and won all of mine. I was very much upset and I think his mother ordered him to return my best ones to me. Another pre-Second World War memory is being in the 'dicky' seat of someone's blue sports car as we sped under the sandstone Northgate of Bridgnorth with the wind whistling past my ears.

During the Second World War my father, as a seed salesman, was in a reserved occupation. He joined the Home Guard rising to the rank of sergeant. I remember him bringing me a flattened halfpenny which he had placed on the railway line when on guard duty. The Home Guard had very little to do, although people were fearful in 1940 of an immediate German invasion. Apparently, one moonlit winter night someone reported a parachute in a field near Bridgnorth and the Home Guard were called out. They surrounded the field which contained a farm building. Nothing happened for two hours. Eventually the farmer who needed his sleep went into the farm building thrashing around with his stick and quickly discovered there was nobody there. The Home Guard soon realised that the 'white parachute silk' seen in the field was a white cow.

I remember making my way with my mother to the sandstone cave in Low Town which served as an air raid shelter. Our town only received two or three bombs from German Luftwaffe pilots intent on shedding their remaining bomb load after a Birmingham or Wolverhampton raid. One bomb completely destroyed The Squirrel, one of our sixty pubs. Fortunately no one was in the building at the time. Another nearly scored a direct hit on my Granny. She lived in a narrow street of terraced houses by St Leonard's Church. A bomb completely destroyed a house opposite killing the lady who lived there. My Granny, who was sheltering in her cellar, emerged unhurt but with her face blackened by coal dust.

During the air raids we usually stayed at home as the town shelter in the sandstone cave was over a mile away. My father and a friend would play darts in the living room and my mother and I would be in the cupboard under the stairs with the door open watching the game and listening for the distinctive sound of a German bomber and then the welcome sound of the siren announcing the 'all clear'.

My father made me a balsa wood model of a Polish fighter plane, its propeller powered by an elastic band. It crashed on its first flight and was badly damaged. My uncle Len, my mother's youngest brother, was in the Royal Air Force and had a serious air crash. He had been a pilot with Imperial Airways before the war and remembered seeing fleets of supposedly civilian aircraft on a Berlin airfield – the future bombing fleet. His plane was badly damaged in a raid over Germany and he was also badly damaged. He visited us in his uniform on crutches with a heavily bandaged leg, an awesome sight for his six-year-old nephew.

The school system was selective. The two elementary schools in Bridgnorth educated students up to the school leaving age of fourteen. At that time it was possible to find work for all school leavers. Some ended up in the Bridgnorth Grammar School which selected their own students for admission at age eleven. After the 1944 Education Act the eleven-plus test was used. In parts of the country there were sufficient grammar school places for only ten per cent of the school population. In Bridgnorth almost a third of those tested could be admitted. This variable percentage of grammar school places created great inequality of opportunity in different areas of the country.

The Bridgnorth Grammar School had traditionally taken its students from mainly middle-class families in the town and sons and daughters of farming families in the surrounding rural area. Many working-class parents considered the grammar school as 'not for us'.

In my own case, my mother did not enrol me at the elementary school but sent me to a little private school housed in the wooden cricket pavilion at the grammar school. The school had a single room with a dividing partition to create two classes. There were two teachers, the head teacher, Miss Foxall, was a devout Baptist who made only modest charges. She had dark hair set in a bun. She was a qualified teacher and ran an efficient and happy school. There was no corporal punishment, just encouragement, and she handed out a mild reproof only rarely. Most people from her school, in this pre-eleven-plus world, went on to the grammar school. Indeed, both my mother's and father's families sent their boys to the grammar school for secondary education. The school had a small boarding facility in the headmaster's house and his wife was the housekeeper. Life in the cricket pavilion was calm and enjoyable and a positive start to my education. Little did the pupils in Miss Foxall's school realise that they had been separated out from most of their contemporaries.

In those wartime days we used slates to write on but also had some lined paper on which we learnt to shape our letters. We learnt to read, write and do arithmetic but had a fairly wide curriculum. I remember being given a saw in order to cut out the shape of a ship's hull. The wood remained intact and I cut my thumb, an early warning of my incompetence in matters of DIY. We performed a play once in front of our parents. I had a non-speaking part as the North Wind in some kind of polar bear costume

In order to get to our school on the playing field we had to enter and leave through the girls' playground of the grammar school. One afternoon in 1941, as we were leaving school and standing at the grammar school gate, a low flying German bomber appeared with swastikas and the iron cross insignia and gaping holes in the wings and fuselage. The pilot was obviously looking for a safe place to make a crash landing. We stood gazing at this sudden apparition but escaped unhurt as he flew west into wilder country.

The school in the cricket pavilion was called 'The Junior Preparatory School at the Grammar School Bridgnorth'. My school reports give some feedback on my early education. In those days there were no national tests, each school, and often each teacher, deployed their own assessments and marking schemes. There were two classes in the school. Class A dealt with juniors and Class B was the infant class. My report for spring term of 1940, just after my sixth birthday, indicated that I was 'thoughtful' during Bible stories. This subject was head of the subject list but there was no immediate impact on my church attendance record. The only occasion I had attended church, though I cannot remember it, was my infant baptism in the Church of England. So far this had also proved to be a church leaving certificate. At the age of ten, for one afternoon only I attended the Sunday school at the Baptist Church. My head teacher taught there and on this sunny summer's day the Sunday school room was musty and my mind was wandering. I could not wait to get out in the sunshine and join my friends in a countryside adventure. Nevertheless all stories, religious or otherwise, gripped my imagination.

In my school reports my reading was described as excellent. From an early age I was devouring books in large quantities. During my time in primary school my mother had a difficult task in satisfying my appetite for books. I was a sickly child and had the full range of German measles, boils, bronchitis and other childhood illnesses. I spent happy hours in bed reading lots of books. There were regular visits from our GP, Dr Rhodes, who addressed me as 'colonel'.

My early school reports were accurate in other respects and the comments could still apply today: 'arithmetic – works quickly' and 'writing – could be more careful'. Later reports include telling verdicts such as 'imaginative, enthusiastic, talkative', and constant references to 'could be tidier'.

The school was about a mile from our house. I walked by myself to school down a road free of traffic, past the workhouse (no genteel name for it in those days), across a merger with the narrow 'main' road between Bridgnorth and Broseley then across the road to the girls' entrance to the grammar school. The final two hundred yard walk on the school site took me past the grammar school building, across the girls' playground and then down a lane which was bordered by an orchard and the school garden. At the end of the lane was the school playing field and our prep school in the wooden pavilion.

I remember one embarrassing journey from school to home when I was six. I was gently admonished for 'messing' my short trousers and was sent home to get cleaned up. I wandered home slowly and played for time by diverting on the way to visit a public playing field. This random dawdling must have extended my walk home by half a mile. I was apprehensive but received a sympathetic hearing at home on my return about an hour later. This was obviously the standard pastoral practice at my school. Today it would have breached health and safety and pupil safeguarding legislation. However, I learnt my lesson and never 'messed' myself again.

When I was seven, my father joined a seed merchant company based in Worcestershire. Only years later did I learn that my mother did not want to leave her home town of Bridgnorth so my father took lodgings in Kidderminster. We saw less and less of him and eventually he met someone else. My parents divorced when I was twelve years old although I continued to see my father once a fortnight in Wolverhampton where we visited a stamp shop (I was a keen philatelist) and then went to the Molineux football ground to support our favourite team Wolverhampton Wanderers (Wolves).

Back in Bridgnorth I enjoyed a happy childhood. I began piano lessons with a good teacher, a blind piano tuner Mr Hopkins who lived 'round the corner' in a private house. For some time I enjoyed my lessons but tuned out at the age of eleven when he introduced me to a Bach fugue. My lessons had made me an adequate busker on the piano. This skill would be useful in later life when I played the piano for a New Year celebration in the village, although this did require manhandling our own upright piano to the pub and back through our Somerset village.

Another activity I tried was membership of the Wolf Cubs. I lasted only six weeks. As part of the initial training I was expected to catch a tennis ball one handed. I am left handed so I got on well with the left hand but with the right I failed miserably and left the organisation after six weeks of seemingly pointless and boring attempts to do the impossible.

Although I was an only child, my social life was busy. I played regularly with Sylvia a girl of my own age who lived just two doors away. Frequently, I walked about a mile to Westgate, a suburban leafy road with private houses. A school friend of mine, John, who lived there, was often away from school because he had a 'bad heart'. The treatment in those days seemed to be bed rest and periodic confinement to his bedroom which became the main playroom. The war was still raging and we decided to invent our own war game. We acquired a large map of the world and made small pieces for our game out of plasticine. We had armies, ships and planes and used dice to determine movements and battle results. At one point the Japanese captured most of Australia in our version of a world war. The game was then refined to include the production of a newspaper which recorded the daily activities of our military forces. The final embellishment was the creation of a new language 'Lotu'. We used this to produce news reports and also included words of Lotu in the occasional letters written to each other when we were on holiday.

Another childhood activity was wandering the wild countryside around our home town. We would play wide games in the tall ferns of the hilly areas on the left bank of the Severn in Low Town and have idyllic cycling expeditions to other towns. The only potentially dangerous excursion was to Ironbridge with its gorge about eight miles from Bridgnorth. This area was the cradle of the industrial revolution. The small industrial communities around Ironbridge were still busy with potteries, coal mines and iron works. We bought lemonade at a small shop then pedalled hard for home. We were afraid of being beaten up by the local lads who had a reputation for defence of their realm.

The only real aggression we experienced was in Bridgnorth itself in a sedate area of private housing. My friend John's brother Dick chased us once with a carving knife and we quickly took flight. Our only other great escape was from an orchard behind John's home. On one occasion, during an intended scrumping expedition, all three of us managed to leap a hedge and escape the jaws of the farmer's dog.

In a sleepy market town, only occasionally touched by war, we were left to our own devices. There were no attempts to organise our free time for us. Parents did not have time or much inclination to play with us and there were no organised leisure pursuits apart from Saturday morning cinema which was a highlight of our week. Those who would do things for us after the war were fully engaged in the war itself or busy on the home front. My mother's efforts on the home front included taking a lodger, Sam, a Lancashire man who worked at the munitions factory and stayed with us from Monday to Friday. My main memory of him is that he always got to my comics, the *Beano* and the *Dandy*, before I had a chance to look at them. *Children's Hour* on the wireless included favourites such as *Toy Town* featuring Larry the Lamb.

During 1945 I sat the eleven-plus exam, a new requirement under the 1944 Education Act. I passed and in September of that year entered the Remove at Bridgnorth Grammar School. Towns seldom founded schools but Bridgnorth Grammar School owed its foundation to an Act of the Corporation in 1503, which established a 'common school'. The school was supported out of the revenues of the Chantries of St Leonards. When chantries were abolished in

1548 money was allocated in perpetuity to ' a Scholemaster kept getting a grammar schole'. A school building was built in St Leonards Close in 1595 and renovated in 1785. A house was built in 1629 to accommodate both the minister of the Church and the headmaster of the school. Later this became a boarding house for the school and still accommodated the headmaster. My father and his brothers were all boarders at the grammar school which provided for boys only.

The 'new' co-educational grammar school had been built in 1910 and was a pleasant campus on the edge of the town with woodland and fields adjacent. The total number of students was 300. Boys and girls met in classrooms, passed each other along the corridors, joined together for school assemblies and had the benefit of occasional school dances. These were preceded by dancing classes for boys and girls in the small school hall where we were taught by our mathematics teacher, Mr Swann, who did a good job to get us to strictly come dancing. The atmosphere was ordered but only fairly relaxed given our shyness.

The headmaster, Mr Barrett, was not a dominant figure around the school. The dominant person was the head of the girls' school, Miss Stewart, a large red-faced serious lady who wore her hair in 'earphones' and ruled in a much less relaxed manner. Sometimes Mr Barrett popped into classes, sat on the teacher's desk and chatted to the pupils. I was sent to him only once for the cane. There was very little bullying but I was occasionally hassled as a thin, weedy boy with glasses when I first arrived in the school. Some older boys behind me started winding me up in assembly, the usual taunts of 'four eyes' predominating. The headmaster listened to my account of the incident. I escaped a caning. What sanction was applied to my tormentors I do not know. There was only one other attack on me by a much taller and fatter boy of my own age. On that occasion, in the playground, he punched me. My immediate reaction was to raise my left arm vertically, make a fist and jump. I made his nose bleed, he burst into tears and to my surprise he never touched me again.

The grammar school, like all others, had suffered the loss of staff due to the wartime enlistment of teachers. Even so, it gathered a range of expertise and personalities who provided a rich and varied experience of the teaching profession in class and in out-of-school activities. Taking what we now consider to be the core subjects, I was taught English by Miss Passey, was a kind and gentle woman who rode her bicycle to school with a basket on the handlebars which always bore a burden of marked exercise books. She had a mild manner, a quiet voice and complete command of every class. She never had to raise her voice or reprimand a pupil. She had a great love of literature and an enthusiasm for it which engaged our attention. She produced plays, mainly extracts from Shakespeare plays. One year I played Macbeth in a sixth form production which was highly charged and dramatic. At the dress rehearsal the girl playing Lady Macbeth got so much into the part that in the murder scene she went into hysterics and had to be calmed down. The phrase that got her was her line: 'who would have thought the old man had so much blood in him?' She recovered for the performance to a live audience the next evening and I still have a photograph of our dramatic efforts. I also remember playing Malvolio in an outdoor production of *Twelfth Night* in the school grounds.

Mathematics was taught by Mr Swann, the ballroom dancing coach, a Cambridge man who had served in the First World War. He was a serious person, clear and precise in his teaching and gave us a good grounding. Again, discipline was good. It fell apart only for one week when he was away and we had a supply teacher who was not up to the task and endured the misery that comes to the inadequate teacher. We thirteen-year-olds had a great week disrupting his classes.

In science we had a varied and contrasting team. The chemistry teacher, another veteran, was known for his dry wit – 'Why did the oxide? Because the ac-id!' For some reason we had to choose to do either chemistry or biology in the third year (Year 9). There was another illogicality for anyone wanting to pursue a medical career – a choice between biology and Latin. I dropped chemistry and Latin. The main motivation was that biology lessons were chaotic and out of control. Years later I learnt from my stepmother that she had been taught years earlier by the same biology teacher in another Shropshire grammar school. That school had obviously passed the parcel to Bridgnorth Grammar School where the same teacher endured even more years of misery. In stark contrast a new physics teacher, Mr Sims, was responsible for firing up my love of that subject. He was young but had already been badly injured in the war. An ex-RAF pilot, his face was badly burnt and scarred but he was an inspirational teacher who loved his subject.

A teacher who had considerable influence on my love of music was Ben Unitt, an RAF ex-serviceman who taught me to play violin and ran the school orchestra. On more than one occasion he and his wife Kay invited students to their home for a musical evening. Performers included Mr Parry, the English teacher who was both an excellent pianist and keen mountaineer. He and all our teachers were people who shared their skills and enthusiasms with us, unconstrained by constant testing and the detailed requirements of an all-embracing and complex national curriculum. Our other teachers made their subjects interesting in a variety of ways. In my first year at the grammar school we had a geography teacher nearing retirement, 'Slosher' Smith. He was an excellent shot with the board rubber. He also told stories, probably tall ones, of his days in the Amazon. In the following year a new geography teacher, Mr Wells, arrived. He was eventually instrumental in persuading me that the best university to go to was his own – Leeds. The history teacher, Miss Paget, was an excellent medieval historian and taught us well although there was sometimes mild class disruption. She came into her own in the sixth form where my friend David Barnes and myself, the only motorcycle owners, were once persuaded to drive our BSA Bantam motorcycles forty miles along remote icy roads to Ludlow and back on a January evening to hear a history lecture at Ludlow Castle. I kept good sixth form history notes which were cartoon drawings but did the job when it came to revision for the Higher School Certificate.

When I was in the fifth form (Year 11) there was a new art teacher who ruined my interest in what had been one of my favourite subjects. I enjoyed drawing landscapes. The new teacher was probably a gifted artist himself but he was volatile, had some class discipline problems and could be crushingly negative about work which he considered sub-standard. My interest in the subject was soon crushed. Students know a good teacher when they see one but often have little patience with those who cannot teach effectively.

We had sat the School Certificate Examination at sixteen and I almost left school at that point. A friend was leaving school to start a business making and selling plaster wall plaques of ducks, a peculiar feature of early 1950s décor. Behind the scenes my grandmother arranged that I should stay on in the sixth form but had I left school at this stage I might have become a successful owner of several fish and chip shops like my friend. My grandmother, a successful business woman, knew better. Plaster wall plaques were a temporary fashion and my friend and I could have ended up like the Americans who were still producing buggy whips at a time when the internal combustion engine was replacing horses.

Our school provided no careers advice. Sixth formers were either destined for university or exceptionally, teacher training. Otherwise many pupils left at sixteen and went back to the family farm or employment in the bank or other local offices. Fortunately this was a time of full employment. At eighteen all boys went off to do National Service unless they applied for deferment in order to go to university.

Our only political education at the grammar school was a mock general election in 1951. We knew the Conservatives would win any election in our school. I was selected as Liberal candidate and beat the Labour and the Communist candidates. This one-off event triggered an interest in politics and I am sure it had a lasting influence on my political views.

2

---

education otherwise – outside school

Up to the age of eighteen other organisations had a hand in my education. My mother and father had divorced in 1946 when I was twelve and my mother sank steadily into depression. I remember frequent occasions when she played the piano and sang a popular song of the time with the poignant words; 'there's nothing left for me, of things that used to be, as I sit here alone among my souvenirs'. I have little recollection of the divorce because my father lived elsewhere and my mother never spoke about it.

The crunch came two years later. My Uncle Les met me as I returned from school to tell me that my mother was seriously ill with a nervous breakdown and was in hospital at Stafford some thirty miles away. She was suffering from schizophrenia and was in that same hospital for three and a half years. Much later in life I learnt that she had had a breakdown in her early twenties. Her illness probably explained her fear of leaving her home town and not joining my father in his new work in Worcestershire. My maternal grandmother always had great sympathy for him, more indeed than his own mother who initially refused to welcome his new wife to the family home at Easthope. In addition, my mother's youngest brother had been killed in a dramatic air crash in Kenya around the time that my parents divorced and that would have had a devastating effect on her.

The impact on my life was immediate. I stayed initially with my uncle and aunt and their family in Low Town but soon transferred to High Town again to stay with my maternal grandmother and her son Les in the terraced house in Church Street near the town centre. This marked a dramatic move for me as I began to participate in a number of community activities that enhanced my education. The 1944 Education Act speaks of the mental, physical, social, cultural and spiritual development of young people. This is where my rounded education was given a further boost.

Granny immediately provided a good return on my basic pocket money by playing cards with me. She enjoyed playing pontoon and rummy for money. The amounts do not sound much now but regular evening sessions would earn me between two old pence and one shilling. I do not think she lost deliberately because she had been a shrewd business woman. I still have the notebook in which I recorded my regular winnings.

Uncle Les had returned from the army in 1946. He had been a sergeant PTI, physical training instructor, working on the rehabilitation of war injured servicemen. He had been trained as a carpet designer before the war. At the end of the war he had wanted to do teacher training but because his younger brother Len had been killed he stayed at home to look after his mother and took a job as a painter and decorator. He was very active in the community. He was a member of St Leonard's Church choir and the male voice choir, played the trombone with the Bridgnorth Silver Prize Band, taught PE as a volunteer at the local Boys' Club and was a member of the ex-servicemen's club – the Comrades Club – and a keen supporter of the Labour Party.

The first thing my uncle did was to encourage me to join the Bridgnorth Boys' Club. The club was based in the oldest house in Bridgnorth, Bishop Percy's House. It was sited at the bottom of the Cartway. This was the original commercial route between High Town and Low Town during the period of the industrial revolution. Barges made their way between Ironbridge Gorge and towns downstream of Bridgnorth as far as Bristol and the sea. Cartway was full of terraced cottages and still had some sandstone cave dwellings faced by brick.

Bishop Percy's House was a half-timbered sixteenth-century building. It was three storeys high and had a large amount of decorative wood in straight and curved lines on the façade. Above the doorway was the following inscription: 'Except the Lord build the Owse the Labourers thereof avail nothing, erected by R for 1580.' R was Richard Forster or Foster. A later resident was Bishop Percy who was born there in 1729 and later educated at Bridgnorth Grammar School. He was the author of *Reliques of Ancient English Poetry* and later became Bishop of Dromore in Ireland. By 1856, the building housed a foundry and a shop, no doubt serving the needs of carters and their horse power. One of Foster's descendants at Apley Hall, Major AW Foster MC, presented the house to the Boys' Club in 1945. It was restored in 1949 not long after I joined the club. I had the job of presenting an illuminated address to Major Foster, and it being my public speaking debut, I almost presented it to the wrong man at the celebration supper. This was a near miss but also encouraged my lifelong love of public speaking.

The restored house offered a very comfortable base for the canteen, the snooker room and various other rooms accessed by twisting uneven staircases. Here we prepared for plays and concerts that were performed at an annual club night in a Low Town parish hall and then taken on tour to some of the local village halls. The house also had bath and shower facilities. Behind it was an old wooden army hut in which my uncle taught gymnastics. We also learnt some boxing and played shinty with walking sticks and a hard puck. In the summer time we did athletics and enjoyed wide games in the woods and high fens near the town. These wide games were devised and run by my uncle and a friend who had been a commando during the war.

There was a junior club starting at age eleven. The senior club admitted boys in the fourteen to eighteen age range. Only a few grammar school boys were in the Boys' Club so a very important part of my club membership was the opportunity to meet up to three evenings a week with those boys who had attended the two elementary schools, St Leonard's (High Town) and St Mary's (Low Town) all of whom had left school and were in work.

Everyone had endured the wartime rationing and blackouts but this was the first time I met boys for whom the Boys' Club supper was their main meal of the day. The canteen was run by some of their mothers. The important leader of the canteen was Mrs Ely a mother of several boys who lived in Cartway. She fed us at a modest price with delights such as beans on toast and cheese and potato pie. A regular pudding was bread pudding, a very popular combination of stale white bread and dried fruit.

In the summer following the School Certificate Examinations I was recruited as a helper on the junior club holiday to Jersey. We went by coach to Southampton and then travelled by boat to the Channel Islands. We noticed that the eleven- and twelve-year-olds were buying cigarettes and cider on board the ferry. The leaders met for a hurried conference on board. 'Don't worry,' said Mrs Ely, 'I'll sort it out at supper time.' We arrived in the early evening at a church hall in Jersey. There was a well-appointed kitchen and the boys were to sleep on palliasses – fairly comfortable straw mattresses. Mrs Ely prepared supper and just before we ate it she made an announcement. 'I noticed on the boat that you boys have already started to buy holiday presents for your mums and dads. We leave this hall each day and we need to keep everything locked up in a safe place. Bring the presents to me after supper and I will make sure that they are kept safe until we get back to Bridgnorth'. This expert bit of child psychology worked wonders and every last purchase was willingly handed over to Mrs Ely.

The influence of volunteers such as Mrs Ely was considerable. In later years I was sad to see that too often the expansion of full- and part-time paid posts meant sometimes losing contact with volunteers who would have shared their skills with young people.

The Boys' Club leader, Fred Mold, was a short, slightly built man. He was disabled, having a 'hunchback', as we then termed scoliosis. He had a little training for the job, was quiet and unassuming but ran a very successful club. He was a good leader managing a diverse group of adult helpers which included ex-army NCOs, factory workers, mothers and one professional solicitor. Years later he would take firm action when it was suspected that one adult was attempting to sexually abuse boys. This person had been a long-standing supporter of the club but Fred asked him to leave immediately. The person concerned lived many miles away from Bridgnorth and we never saw him again.

Fred was brilliant at giving boys responsibility and developing their leadership skills. In my own case he encouraged me to help organise the juniors. I wrote and produced sketches for the juniors' concerts and helped out on club holidays. I also helped to organise wide games and athletics events. Fred encouraged me to play my violin and take part in comedy acts and one-act plays in our concert parties. I was introduced to committee work by Fred and became chairman of the Boys' Club committee.

All this was done during my time at Bridgnorth Grammar School where I was active in school plays, played violin in the school orchestra, was a member of school football and cricket teams and occasionally put my mind to some academic work. I became a school prefect. This was not the full story of my hyperactivity which was experienced by both school and community organisations.

Music was becoming an important part of my life and included an introduction to another instrument, the trombone. Soon after I moved to my Granny's house I accompanied Uncle Les to the upper room of the Comrades Club in High Town where the Bridgnoth Silver Prize Band held their practices. Uncle Les introduced me to Joe Key, the bandleader. He had been trained at the Army School of Music at Kneller Hall and had played in the Grenadier Guards Band. The Bridgnorth Silver Prize Band occasionally entered competitions but it also played almost every week in the summer time at village fetes and also in numerous pub gardens on Sunday afternoons. Joe tried me on the tenor trombone, my uncle's chosen instrument, but he decided my mouth was too big. I am sure this diagnosis was shared by many people who encountered me using my mouth in a variety of contexts. I was handed the bass trombone. It was very large, silver in colour and had a handle which was used to extend the slide. I enjoyed the band practices.

The band had several young members and I was delighted to find myself in a co-education context. I soon got to know Olive, a brilliant cornet player around my age. I still have a blurred black and white photo of us, me with my arm around her waist in the decorous manner of 1949. I was pleased for Olive but otherwise very disappointed when she went away to become a member of the prestigious Ivy Benson Jazz Band.

There was another benefit of band membership which I enjoyed; we played at pubs on Sunday afternoons in the summer. Part of the enjoyment was the availability of beer to moisten hard working lips. The band members drank mainly mild beers, lager not having been discovered by our pubs at this stage. The younger, underage members of the band were permitted a pint of shandy – two thirds beer, one third lemonade. I do not know where this concession came from. No one questioned it. Perhaps our bandmaster had some special influence over the pub owners.

Our band was once invited to undertake a most important municipal task. It would be a great honour for the band and a chance to demonstrate our skill before the whole town. The Freedom of the Borough of Bridgnorth was to be given to Kings Shropshire Light Infantry. On the big day when they arrived to march down the High Street with flags flying and bayonets fixed, we were to accompany them playing the regimental march. We practised the march for some weeks. It was an old Shropshire hunting tune called 'Old Towler', the name of a once famous foxhound. This title should have given us early warning of what was about to happen. The officers of the regiment arrived for the parade on horseback. It suddenly struck us that this was going to be a challenge for those playing and carrying heavy instruments. At that point we realised the relevance of an instruction that told us the regiment marched at one hundred and forty paces to the minute. We all lined up behind the battalion and the order was given to 'Quick March' and the light infantry set off at a world beating pace accompanied by the trotting horses of the officers. The band kept up to start with but just as we entered the arch of the Town Hall in the middle of the High Street, lined by cheering crowds, the man playing the heavy B flat bass peeled off saying in effect he would serve no more. We lost one or two other pieces of our heavy artillery but I am proud to say that the trombones, cornets and tenor horns of the band's lightweight infantry made it all the way.

Another musical opportunity soon presented itself at the Bridgnorth Comrades Club. On a Saturday night in the large smoke-filled upstairs bar members and their wives would sit at tables. In one corner of the room was a small stage with a piano where the pianist, Barry Batkins, a man with curly black hair and an RAF style moustache, used to entertain on a Saturday night. He needed an instrument to accompany him, so every Saturday evening for some time I would bring along my violin to play popular tunes by ear. The two instruments together made a bearable sound and the customers often burst into some of the old favourites of yesteryear and more modern numbers such as 'Whispering Grass' and 'Night Riders in the Sky'. I was paid five shillings a night, well below Musicians' Union rates but a fortune for me and a free pint of shandy came along as an added incentive. I even accompanied Barry on one occasion as he played in one of the Low Town pubs.

My urban upbringing was complemented by the rural branch of the family. My father's family had a great influence on my life from an early age. Before my parents were divorced we visited Easthope Cottage Farm on the Wenlock Edge quite frequently. The farm was in the small village of Easthope where the family were strong supporters of the parish church. The front lawn of the farmhouse, a Georgian six bedroom property, overlooked a small meadow which usually held sheep. Just beyond the far hedge of the meadow was the churchyard where several generations of the family were buried. The rector, Father Ball, was a very frail parson who was in his nineties. He was unmarried but had a housekeeper and some help with the rectory garden. His gardener and odd job man Dick was also ancient. Each autumn they used to cut logs for the rectory fires. They used a crosscut saw. It was a fine sight to see them sawing away, neither wanting to admit they needed a rest.

Easthope was an exciting place for a small child. My paternal grandparents were a little detached but we received no-nonsense care from my Cheshire-born Grandma Olive whose job in life was to keep us well fed and warm. Grandad Richard sat most of the time by the kitchen range, peering myopically through pebble glasses. He was short sighted and probably had cataracts as well. Thank you, Grandad, for that part of my inheritance. He ventured out occasionally into the farmyard for minor duties. In some ways the farm came to him. A cade, an orphaned lamb, would be brought into the house to be fed warm milk from a bottle. The milk was heated up on the kitchen stove. Occasionally a small lamb would be put into the warming oven for a time, a kind of temporary metallic womb. I was allowed to help with feeding a lamb and was amazed that this cuddly woollen creature had a head as hard as that on a drunken head-butt specialist.

My father, Edward, had left the farm so my uncle, George, the second of four sons, managed the farm which comprised one hundred and fifty acres of arable, pasture, woodland and hills. There were sheep, cattle and also at any

one time some two thousand poultry. I used to accompany
Uncle George to the milking parlour. I helped to give warm
milk to the security guards – the half-feral cats who kept the
rats and mice under control in the farm buildings. When I
was a little older I helped to pour the milk from the buckets
into churns via the cooler. The churns would be collected
daily by the milk lorry.

The army of fowl belonged to my Uncle Henry who
had a wonderful sense of humour. I helped him to take a
broody hen into solitary confinement from time to time.
He said he was putting them into prison so that they would
reform and start laying. It was a wonderful sight for a child
to see hundreds of chicks in a farm building near the house
being warmed up by radiant lamps and providing a loud
cheery chicken orchestra.

I used to hang out with other children of the village. We
wandered round the fields with no specific purpose in mind
but always looking out for berries or animals. Occasionally
I accompanied my Uncle George on an autumn evening
setting snares for the rabbits in the wood. The purpose was
to catch them for the pot. I did not enjoy the result of our
efforts when a rabbit was partially trapped and injured but it
was speedily dispatched by Uncle George. At harvest time I
also played my part in the rabbit hunt. I and other boys from
the village would have sticks and watch as the horse team
gradually cut the corn, moving from the edge of the field to
the centre. Everyone in the village helped with the harvest.
They were fuelled by cider made on the farm, apart from
those who preferred to bring their own bottle of cold tea.
As the area of cover became smaller, rabbits would break

out and make a run for it. It was our job to catch them for the pot if we could. I cannot remember catching any at all. Perhaps the aim was to keep us occupied and out of the way of the harvesting team.

Another country task was building the hayrick. At the age of seven I was helping one day to build a rick and I was given my own full size 'pikel'. This was a two pronged pitchfork with which we bundled and moved the hay. The inevitable happened. I took an enthusiastic stab at the hay and drove one prong of the fork straight through my foot. The emergency services moved into action at once. Uncle George pulled out the prong quickly and carried me up to the farmhouse and my grandma immediately washed the wound, applied lots of iodine and bandaged it all up. There was no need to call a doctor and, surprisingly, I quickly recovered. Our family was of Norwegian ancestry and I suppose this was a good example of the Viking ability to take a hit, mop up the blood and keep on stabbing.

Another country pursuit was late night courting with a chaperone. I remember walking along the road on Wenlock Edge itself, on a dark night with Uncle George who went to visit his fiancée Muriel on a farm about a mile away. In those days, when there was no television and a war was on, these country pursuits continued unabated. Young farmers were in a reserved occupation but were by no means reserved in seeking out a future wife. Eventually I attended the wedding of George and Muriel at Easthope Church with a reception at the farm. The new bride soon played her part in running the farm and eventually George succeeded his father. Muriel was a fabulous pudding maker but strong willed. She would say, 'Can you manage more pudding?' The reply usually was 'No thank you, Auntie.' At this she would say, 'Oh yes you can,' and pile up the plate again.

My country relatives did so much to enrich my childhood and the love of the countryside particularly the wildlife, the hills and high places had a lasting effect on me and the simple faith and lifestyle of the family had an impact on me when I reached the age at which young adults start to think about themselves and their place in the world. Around the age of sixteen, as is usual in adolescence, I started to think about the meaning of life and decided that while churches were boring there was certainly a good case to make for a creator of the universe. My Uncle Les had attended St Leonard's Church for years. He was in the choir but suggested I might like to look in on a service. The rector, Wallace Cox, was a friendly and dynamic personality. He had two sons a little older than I was but much of the time they were away at school. Nevertheless I got drawn in to the church to the stage where I was confirmed in the Church of England at the age of seventeen. Soon after I was asked to read lessons and finally invited to help take services. In later years this would lead to being asked by the Bishop of Hereford to take services for two Methodist circuits in Shropshire. I soon became experienced at delivering an address from the pulpit.

Circumstances changed suddenly when I was seventeen. I was happily established in my very busy life aided and abetted by school, club, town band, church, athletics and other sporting activities. To this could be added paid work as a Saturday night fiddle player. The news came that my mother was returning home from hospital. For three and a half years I had visited her every other Saturday in hospital at Stafford. This required a journey by bus, changing at Wolverhampton, a whole day trek. I was very concerned that my mother's release from hospital would disrupt my busy and happy local life or even thwart my plans to go to university.

My parents' divorce and my mother's long-term illness could have had a very negative effect on my young life. Since my mother's admission to mental hospital when I was fourteen I had lived with my grandmother and enjoyed a positive and active life at school and in the community, My grandmother had provided a secure springboard for me to grow up and explore new experiences. I was apprehensive when I learned that my mother would be released from hospital. It would have been easy to defer my departure from Bridgnorth and seek a job locally but this did not even occur to me. I would have to leave either for National Service or university at eighteen. I had already deferred my National Service until after university and all had seemed settled. However my mother returned to Bridgnorth and later, when I had finished university and was in the Royal Air Force, my mother would suffer with her mental illness again.

Even so, in later years, my wife, Gill, was always aware that I was anxious about my mother's mental health. From university I phoned my mother every Sunday, worried that I might find her unwell. I had to commit her to hospital again in 1957, when I was serving in the RAF, and again in 1960, when I was a youth officer in Shrewsbury. Thereafter therapeutic drugs improved and she never had to return to hospital again. In 1978 my mother came to live next door to Gill and myself in Somerset. Gill cared for her for the last twelve months of her life. She would join us for meals, she saw much of the grandchildren and Gill would encourage her to play our piano in the afternoon.

Only later in life did I reflect upon the difficulties my mother had experienced throughout her life. My own self-interest and hyperactivity had certainly shielded me from reflecting on the problem of her illness during my formative years. It was after my mother had died that I began to fully understand the nature of her illness and its causes. She had been in Australia at the age of four when her father died there. A visit to Australia in her early twenties to meet friends in Melbourne where he had died had triggered her illness and she had been in hospital after her return to England. This was a few years before meeting my father. The death of her youngest brother in an air crash might have triggered her long stay in hospital when I was still at school.

In all, I do not consider my childhood and youth to have been unhappy or deprived. During the war parents were not as closely engaged with their children as they are nowadays. The absence of fathers at war, war work and the billeting of workers or evacuees meant that I and my friends were free to amuse ourselves as we wished. In wartime there were no leisure activities organised for us. If anything we had the freedom that some people now recommend for children – time out to be themselves and even an element of real risk to be introduced to play facilities. Children now face other problems such as the all-pervasive desire of adults to fill the child's 'spare' time with study or 'useful' activities.

The friends I chose, my family, school and various community groups all had a hand in my development through childhood and adolescence. My home life had been disrupted but I was given new experiences, rich in warm friendships and exciting opportunities to discover and develop my own skills. I was clearly a child in need of safeguarding and I consider myself very fortunate to have had the support of school, family and voluntary community leaders who gave me a rich exposure to new interests and challenges.

My early education was not governed by a national curriculum or an effective school inspection regime. Our teachers had high status in the community. The Bridgnorth Grammar School provided a range of extra-curricular opportunities and an incompetent teacher was both an entertainment and a rarity. The situation was different for the friends who did not pass the eleven-plus. Their extra-curricular activities were few and at the age of fourteen many of them were at work. Curiously, not only did I benefit from my grammar school but was also able to share the friendship and activities of friends who had been to the two elementary schools in the town. By accident I was the recipient of a socially comprehensive education.

3

---

wider horizons – sixth form, university and extended national service

When I entered the sixth form it was assumed that I would go on to higher education. I would be the first person in my family to go to university. Only the availability of state and means tested county scholarships made such a choice possible.

Many of my contemporaries had already left school to start work, in the banking or accountancy professions or in the family business. The school honours board reflected the paucity of numbers going on to higher education, two or three people a year were so honoured. This was not surprising as nationally only about five percent of students went on to university at this time. Many of the names on the honours board were those of people following the family tradition in medicine, law or teaching. Certainly no one in my family had even thought of going to university. I am sure that this was not the case in large grammar schools, however, in this small market town serving a large rural catchment (recruitment) area the majority of those who attended the grammar school already had jobs lined up for them or took vocational and professional routes which did not demand a university degree. My knowledge of universities was negligible.

During my second year in the sixth form I was inspired by my history teacher, Miss Paget, to apply to read history at her alma mater, King's College London. King's required all history students to have Latin. The snag was that at the age of thirteen I had decided to drop Latin in order to enjoy a regular opportunity to join in the enjoyable pastime of disrupting biology lessons. I attempted to pass School Certificate Latin in one term and failed. I had not curtailed my extensive social life so this was not surprising. As second choice I heeded my geography teacher's advice and was offered a place at the University of Leeds to read a General Honours degree course covering three subjects, English, geography and history. I secured a place and a County Scholarship. I went off to university just after my mother returned home from three and a half years in hospital. In one sense, university was an escape from the fear that I would be tied down as an only child to caring for a mentally fragile single parent.

It was with great excitement that I set off by bus and train to enrol at the University of Leeds. My first real experience of a northern city was Sheffield, viewed through a train window which showed the glowing fires of blast furnaces and a lot of smoke and greyness. Leeds was less smoky around the city. I dragged my large suitcase onto a Leeds tram, another new experience, and travelled to Headingley and my new home, Devonshire Hall. The Hall was in a quiet suburban road well provided with trees which were sooty from the prevailing smog that dominated industrial cities before the smoke abatement acts.

Devonshire Hall had been designed and built in the 1930s on the lines of an Oxbridge college. The Porter's Lodge was at the entrance to a quadrangle flanked by residential blocks at each side and faced by the main building which contained the dining hall, the bar and various other facilities including squash courts. I was booked in at the Porter's Lodge and taken to R block which held the oldest rooms and had the coke stoves beneath them which provided the central heating. My room, R16, was immediately above the coke fuelled boiler which provided a gentle but permanent chemical ambience to the room. One of my friends from Catalonia would find employment in Hall during vacations. He kept the boiler going during the first winter vacation. One morning the warden of Hall felt cold and stormed in to the cellar to find Jose Selva poking the fire. 'Give me the poker,' cried the warden and Jose accidentally thrust the hot end into the Warden's hand.

Devonshire Hall provided accommodation for a hundred and twenty male students from twenty-eight nations and diverse backgrounds. I shared a room with Bernard Brown from a small town in Suffolk. He was on a State Scholarship and had come up to read English but in freshers week had made an impulsive switch to law. This decision gave him an enjoyable career which culminated in his work as Professor of Law in the University of Auckland, New Zealand. We soon met a new friend, Sid. His full name was Sahidudahar Khan Mohammed. His father owned a leather factory in what was then East Pakistan and Sid was studying for a degree in the textile department. He had been involved in occasional student disturbances in Dacca, his home town, and was an expert knife thrower. Once I was sitting reading in our room when Sid planted a perfect shot about an inch from my left ear as an example of his great skill, which almost matched the expertise of my board-rubber throwing geography teacher.

Living in a diverse international community was a marvellous experience however in the four years I was there we witnessed a dreadful example of racial discrimination. Two Afrikaans South African students were often unkind to another of our friends who was Cape Coloured. Little did we know the anguish he must have endured, because a year after our arrival we were appalled to hear that he had committed suicide during the summer vacation. Otherwise this diverse community got on well and was tolerant and welcoming. One friend, Ayo Afolabi, was a Yoruba from Western Nigeria. He described the Yoruba joy of debate and he chose to read law. Another Nigerian friend, Clement Onymolukwe, was an engineer student from the east of Nigeria. He ended up in an important role in the energy industry there. Years later their respective homelands were, for a time, enemies in the Biafran war. At Devonshire Hall we were friends irrespective of race, or religious or political allegiance.

Our warden, Commander David Hywel Evans, an Oxford man, endeavoured to run the Hall like an Oxford College or perhaps a well-ordered ship. His only rule was that we should 'behave as gentlemen'. We were given the full treatment: short undergraduate gowns to be worn at formal dinner in Hall on Wednesdays, Latin grace, a much truncated one, and an encouragement of Hall activities: cricket, soccer and rugby teams and a choir which performed carols and had its own signature choir number 'Hail Smiling Morn'. Otherwise we were left to our own devices.

About half of the students came straight from school, others had completed their National Service. For example, Geoff, who was reading a degree in social sciences, had just completed his National Service as an officer in the Royal Artillery. At dead of night in R block when some of us were in our rooms strange sounds might be heard. Geoff, who had a marvellous sense of humour, would amuse us with sounds of baby talk coming from his room. There was also a group of older ex-servicemen some of whom had war service. They were richer than the impoverished scholarship students who had come straight from school and enjoyed a lively social life in the Hall and university union bars.

There were residential halls for women in Leeds. We were allowed to visit them for afternoon tea on Wednesday afternoons. There were many other extra-curricular opportunities to meet and on occasion students managed longer visits. There was once a very intrusive visit after-hours. A group of engineering students managed to remove a complete toilet bowl from a women's hall without discovery.

Before I arrived at Leeds in October 1952 I had become a Christian and was soon sought out by two organisations: the Student Christian Movement (SCM) which focuses on international social issues and the Leeds University Christian Union (LUCU) which was conservative in its biblical approach. I managed to become a member of both but as time went on I took an active part in LUCU and became its president in my finals year because the preferred candidate wisely withdrew to concentrate on his science finals. I believe he ended up with a distinguished career in the Labour Party in the north of England. His decision to decline to lead LUCU was a wise academic decision and showed great political acumen. The SCM offered a different focus based upon Christian involvement in social affairs rather than individual development.

The traditions promoted by Devonshire Hall did not influence the administration of the general degree arrangements. There was no fully developed tutorial system on the Oxbridge model. In my first year I found myself with plenty of spare time. I was reading a General Honours course, in English, geography and history with first year philosophy as an additional subject. For this I had no tutorials and was required to attend a total of seven lectures a week. My studies almost became a leisure activity. The study of three subjects was too superficial, the geography was boring for me in that it majored on the economic geography of the region.

English was much more entertaining. There was occasional tutorial work and the ability of one eminent academic to relate everything to Marxist analysis was good fun. It was history that interested me most and was in the end my most successful area of study. I concluded at the time that I would rather have concentrated on history and this is what I tended to do. The result was inevitable. I achieved a pass which I was told informally included a First in history. It was a total lack of attention to geography and an excess of student activity that did for me.

I was displaying a typical adolescent immaturity. I dabbled in many things during my three years as an undergraduate. I played some hockey for the university Third Team and also ran in cross-country events. I played cricket, soccer and on one occasion rugby for Hall. I had a walk-on part for two university stage productions. I became business manager of the university journal *The Gryphon* and enjoyed the task of persuading the business community of Leeds to buy advertising space in it. I learnt how to deal with the Yorkshire business war-cry: 'How much?' During my three years the Christian Union provided a Saturday night 'squash' or social meeting in the home of a chemistry professor. All my extra-curricular activities did little for my degree course but they provided excellent employment skills. I did plenty of public speaking in churches and in the open air, including practice at handling hecklers. I learnt the skills of selling to reluctant buyers and I developed my organisational skills.

After the shock of the finals result I enrolled for the Graduate Certificate in Education course at Leeds and stayed on in Hall for a fourth year. I put aside all other activities and threw myself into overdrive on education studies. I had no idea whether or not I would seek a teaching career but I was immediately engaged in both the theoretical and practical aspects of the course. Overall, teaching was good in the university education department with only one exception, an education historian who used his own book and nothing else as the basis for his lectures. His opening words were invariably, 'today my lecture will be based on chapter x of my book from page y to page z'. Otherwise I enjoyed my studies immensely. I withdrew from extra-curricular distractions and enjoyed all aspects of the course.

I had two periods of teaching practice. The first was in a boys' secondary modern school in Harehills, Leeds, in November and December of 1955. The age range was eleven to fifteen. Many of the boys were from working class homes and the school had been difficult for some teachers. At the end of my six weeks I was told that a third form (Year 9) class I taught regularly had trampled on an inadequate teacher the previous term. This may explain the variety of disciplinary practices I saw in action. The class teacher of this particular group ruled by fear. He used a ruler to strike boys on the end of their fingers. This might happen up to ten times in a lesson. I was pleased that I was able to teach the same class without resorting to physical punishment. My lesson notes are very detailed and I remember engaging the class positively. I had to teach mathematics, English, history and some religious education lessons. On one occasion in an RE lesson I was describing the siege of Jerusalem. As I said, 'the siege ladders fell against the city walls,' a window cleaner's ladder hit the external classroom wall. This had an electrifying effect on the class! It was a great confidence booster to succeed in my teaching and my control of the class. I discovered that a well-prepared lesson providing challenge and active involvement of pupils worked well, as did a firm, consistent, but friendly relationship with the class and individuals. Domination and punishment achieved nothing but fear and resentment. The detailed and well-ordered lesson notes which I have to this day are evidence of the attention to detail and impact that I sought.

My second teaching practice was near Pudsey. In those days the town suffered from the smoke of industry and was described as the place where, 't'crows fly backwards to keep t'muck out of their eyes'. The school was not in the smoke but at nearby Fulneck in fresh Yorkshire country air. It was an independent boarding school for boys which also took day boys from the local community and was a Moravian Church foundation. The Moravian Church seemed to be somewhat like an Anglican Church but with greater liturgical choices. My six weeks of teaching practice in the spring term of 1956 provided some new challenges. I was able to teach boys in all secondary year groups up to and including their fifth form (Year 11). Students were neatly dressed in their school uniforms and there were no problems with classroom behaviour. Even out of school the pupils were polite and friendly. I taught history, English and some religious education for those about to sit the GCE religious education examination that summer. The RE teacher, Bishop Connor, a Moravian bishop, had to go to Tibet to ordain some Moravian Church ministers. He left me details of the syllabus to be covered and bade me a cheerful goodbye. He was due to return just as my teaching practice ended. I still have a copy of the detailed report I prepared for him at the end of the six weeks of my teaching practice which outlined the work covered and my assessment of likely results at GCE. I had looked at the mock examination results with the headmaster and we agreed that three pupils should be advised to drop RE, two others were considered doubtful unless their English language skills improved and I declared some others to be difficult to assess accurately. I never enquired about the actual results. By now any of my mistaken predictions are buried somewhere in the school archives.

My dissertation, handed in towards the end of the course in May 1956, was, 'The Teaching of Poetry to Boys in the Secondary Modern School'. I had been impressed with the responsiveness to education by pupils whose capabilities to learn had not been discovered by their own teachers. I had also discovered that those written-off by the selective system at eleven were capable of more. In my teaching practice at Harehills, with the opportunity to teach poetry, I found pupils showed great interest in the subject if the material was presented well. Choral speaking was popular when humorous or onomatopoeic material was introduced and involved the whole class in dramatic rendition. The received wisdom of research at the time was that poetry reading and drama were unpopular in schools. I was pleased to find a much readier response to poetry when the material and presentation were in tune with the pupils' idea of enjoyment.

In reading for my dissertation on the teaching of poetry I was disappointed to find that much of the research was based on the findings of earlier researchers. I discovered that one accepted finding was based on an original idea in a research paper of 1911, and was regurgitated at regular intervals without any additional research being done. This gave me a healthy scepticism about received wisdom which has a strong foothold in accepted 'wisdoms' but is devoid of good action research in schools.

The Graduate Certificate course included a choice of leisure activities that might be shared with pupils in one's future career. I chose rock climbing and canoeing. During the year I had a chance to help out on a Batley Grammar School course at a residential centre in the Lake District. This gave me some experience of leading groups and was invaluable in my later career. In June 1956, another student and I spent a week camping and canoeing down the River Wye from Glasebury to Chepstow.

The result of this year of 'conversion' to academic work and enjoyable teaching practices led to a significant change of fortune in examination results. The pass list had three categories Division I, Division II and recommendation for qualified teacher status. In the total of over a hundred students five of us, myself included, were awarded Division I with distinction in Part 1 (Theory). This result was not to be put into practice in a school because I was now due to do my National Service. I had gained experience of teaching a potentially disruptive class in an inner city secondary modern school over a six week period and had also enjoyed responsibility for managing and teaching a GCE subject in a private school with the blessing of a bishop and a head teacher.

National Service was in one sense a two-year period of compulsory training and work experience. It was not necessarily tailor-made to meet individual needs. In my own case I opted to seek a commission to do three years as a regular rather than two years as a national serviceman.

My first choice of service was the Royal Navy. I had always been interested in ships even though my home town was ninety miles from the sea. This preference for the navy was partly inspired by my mother's second cousin in Poole who had served as a lieutenant commander in the Royal Naval Voluntary Reserve, the 'wavy navy'. He had taken just a few minutes when I was twelve to teach me to swim in the sea. He took me to Durdle Door in Dorset where the sea bed shelved steeply, escorted me into deep water then released me to swim ashore. Had the tactic not worked no doubt he would have rescued me and tried again. The next step in my search for a naval career had occurred at the age of fourteen when I sat the entrance examination for Dartmouth. I developed tonsillitis which was in full spate when I took the exam. I failed to gain a place. In the summer of 1956, I took the intelligence test required of all who were interested in applying for a commission in the services and passed. A friend of mine failed because the registration number of his motorcycle appeared in a mathematical test and he was so mesmerised by it that he failed to complete the questions.

In accordance with my wishes I went to Liverpool for preliminary selection for the Supply Branch of the Royal Navy. I fell at the first physical test where, without my glasses, I was unable to see either a red or a green light in the distance. I can see that this could have caused navigational problems.

The next try was for the Royal Air Force as a ground officer in the Education Branch. I passed and was selected for entry to the Officer Cadet Training Unit. In September 1956 I proceeded by train and ship to Jurby on the Isle of Man. This was to be my home for three months where ground officer cadets, referred to colloquially as 'penguins' were trained. I enjoyed the experience and then went on to RAF Grantham for six weeks to be prepared for duty as an education officer.

I applied for a posting to Singapore and some humourist in the RAF Records Office had me posted to RAF Credenhill, near Hereford. This was in Technical Training Command and accommodated the RAF School of Catering and also the RAF School of Administration which trained personnel of the Women's Royal Air Force (WRAF).

I was in the small education department which served the permanent staff. The work was varied and interesting. Every Monday afternoon I took the train to Great Malvern in order to monitor the work of a flight sergeant who was doing A level geography in preparation for resettlement in civilian life. On other days I took part in resettlement interviews, a kind of careers interview, and helped to manage the station library and classrooms. In these I did some teaching and this included trying to help a leading aircraftsman (LAC) to get his RAF Test Part 1 which would lead to advancement to the rank of corporal. This was about his third attempt. One of my general duties was flight commander of the Catering Flight. Once a week I led them on parade. There was more of a soft shoe shuffle than a tramp of boots as some slightly overweight but very successful chefs underwent this rather irksome weekly exercise. As orderly officer I had to take care of camp security from time to time. The most common task was to look out for liaisons between airmen and the attractive WRAF recruits on a station which had many secluded corners and some mature trees and bushes.

After a few months at Hereford I had to seek a compassionate posting to my home town of Bridgnorth. I was informed that my mother was ill again and I had to have her committed to a mental hospital. RAF Bridgnorth was a recruit training camp. Again, it was not Singapore but it provided plenty of opportunities for me. I was posted to the station Education Department which served the regular staff who trained the constantly changing hordes of National Service recruits who came to Bridgnorth for their basic training. The squadron leader in charge of the station Education Department was due to retire from a long career in the Royal Air Force. Each day he disappeared to the Officers' Mess for lunch, some of it liquid. He was generally absent in the afternoons but was always back on duty punctually at 0800 the next morning. This left a flight lieutenant and myself, by now a flying officer who could not fly, in charge of the unit much of the time.

The Education Department had a library, a classroom, and also interview facilities which were used mainly for resettlement interviews for those returning to civilian life. We provided tutorial support and advice for those who wanted to improve their vocational qualifications. Others were regulars doing correspondence courses in various academic subjects. Our support was always available although sometimes I was only a page or two ahead of the learners in subjects such as GCE physics. There were sometimes other duties. On one occasion I was asked to give a lecture to the Wives Club. Each school holiday we also ran voluntary classes in English and maths for children of service families at the station. This was very enjoyable and we had great fun teaching children who were keen to learn. All of those who came were primary school pupils. I do not remember any liaison with the local schools and although they only attended for one or two weeks, generally mornings, we managed to consolidate their basic skills. We used a variety of activities and games as part of our work with them.

Most days the workload in the afternoons was light though not as inactive as the squadron leader's après midi regime. I was tasked with developing training opportunities for national servicemen who were promising athletes. These included at one point the British Commonwealth javelin champion. The athletes were given a lot of time practising their skills while the main body of recruits continued with more square bashing drills. In the winter I organised cross-country runs for the top athletes. The course was beautiful. Our station was at the top of the escarpment above the woods and sandstone cliff, High Rock, which bordered the left bank of the River Severn. I had access to as many markers as I needed. National Service recruits volunteered in their dozens to mark the course. This meant standing, sitting or lounging for an hour or so in the woods, with stunning views of the Severn Valley, and directing the runners. Marking offered release from the hardships of recruit training.

I was a member of the officers' mess where on formal occasions we put into practice the social graces taught at Jurby, such as passing the port to the left and not draining the bottle in one go. More exciting activities took place later in the evening. One squadron leader was a Polish count. He had been in the Polish Cavalry and had charged the German tanks when they invaded Poland. He then transferred to the Polish Air Force, escaped to Britain and joined the RAF. With sofas in position as hedges he demonstrated a Polish Cavalry charge complete with commands and drawn sabre.

I established a ten-mile road race at Bridgnorth, open to civilian athletes from around the country. This initiative was backed enthusiastically by the RAF station commander who provided funds for trophies. I also helped to found the Bridgnorth Athletic Club. I could not have undertaken these great athletic initiatives without the help of a National Service Corporal Bandsman, Dave Coward. He was a good athlete, an excellent organiser and could fix any problem. After his National Service he emigrated to Canada and apparently within six months became a leading light in one of the oldest athletics clubs in Canada, the Gladstone Club of Toronto.

I had an additional responsibility as flight commander of the RAF Regiment Detachment. The regiment were called the Rock Apes because of their brave defence of Gibraltar during the Second World War. Their task was to defend our airfield. I had to lead them on parade. The sound behind me was completely different from my previous posting, instead of the Hereford soft shoe shuffle I heard the steady, relentless clump of highly polished boots. One morning in the absence of our group captain the wing commander administration took the salute. He gave the command, 'Parade, three paces sideways, march!' The result was chaos as recruits and a few regulars moved left or right or dithered. I am proud to say the regiment stood as firm as the Rock of Gibraltar until a proper order was given.

I was orderly officer one night when we received warning of an armed raid by the Irish Republican Army (IRA). At that time, in the 1950s, the IRA were seeking to steal weapons from military bases. I called out the guard and proceeded to the armoury. The guard were mainly national servicemen. I asked the armourer to issue rifles. He refused, 'Sorry Sir, I am instructed not to issue recruits with rifles, they can use pick axe handles.' I called the duty officer, a squadron leader, who came down to the armoury and was also refused. He then telephoned the commanding officer who came down to the armoury. I think he threatened to shoot the armourer himself or otherwise gain forced entry if guns and ammunition were not released at once, so we were now armed. I carried a Sten gun. I am proud to say that in my officer training I was a marksman with a Sten. The gun itself had been mass produced during the war and was notoriously unreliable. If struck on the floor of a lorry accidentally it could fire automatic rounds through the roof. This was a cold, starry January night with no moon and I hoped it would operate efficiently. There was some snow on the ground and a lot on the hangar roofs. Our first alert came when the orderly sergeant was suddenly struck from behind by a heavy weapon. It turned out to be a lump of snow from a roof. We searched the airfield thoroughly and found nothing except one suspicious car on the road bordering the airfield. This turned out to contain a courting couple. Finally, we stood the guard down at dawn. My only potential active service was a false alarm.

Towards the end of my three years I was asked to apply for a permanent commission in the RAF Regiment. I might have done so had their role remained active. This was now changing in emphasis and became wider. The regiment would be required to be ready for atomic warfare which was now seen as the greatest threat. My role would be potentially suicidal, crawling around an airfield after an attack measuring levels of radiation. I did not see a long-term future in the regiment.

I then had a telephone call from Shrewsbury. The County Youth Officer, Jim Knight, asked me to consider applying for a job as a youth officer. I had met Jim when I was a volunteer helper at the Bridgnorth Boys' Club. I decided to apply but first I would need to learn to drive a car. My existing vehicle was a Corgi Commando motorcycle, a very low slung vehicle. In the winter riding up to camp wearing a greatcoat I looked like a moving apparition with no feet and no obvious means of propulsion. My driving test went well. I was sent to an army airfield base at Lichfield. I was told to take a packet of cigarettes as a present for the examiner should he declare me qualified. On arrival, he asked me to drive round the empty airfield for practice and pointed out one or two errors. We then went round again and returned to his office. He gave me my licence. I had passed. I thanked him and handed over the cigarettes. The result was twofold.

I got the Youth Service job then drove like a maniac for a year or so before reaching a passable standard.

My extended National Service had a considerable influence on the direction of my career in civilian life. I had experienced management responsibility in education and I was not sure that I was ready to be directed again by someone else in a secondary school subject department setting. Furthermore, I enjoyed teaching the service children occasionally but was also well-pleased with my experiences of adult education. Resettlement interviews, tutoring adults engaged in academic courses, organising events both in the RAF and civilian life; the creation of a new athletics club and training other people had all caused me to look wider at careers other than secondary school teaching. My work as a reader in the Church of England and as a preacher on loan in Methodist circuits in Shropshire made me consider ordination. I attended a potential chaplain's course at Dowdeswell Manor in Gloucestershire but the experience confirmed that I did not want to turn my collar round and be a full-time minister.

I had never definitely set my sights on a specific career and the groundwork for a serendipitous career path was laid by the Royal Air Force who reinforced my multiple skills. I was now able to respond to the invitation and launch a youth service challenge which offered a pay rise from £620 to £708 a year, a car, a telephone/postage allowance and a part-time secretary as the perks of the job.

4

———

home county – new challenge and youth work

My formal interview for the post of youth officer for Central Shropshire was at County Hall Shrewsbury early in 1959. There were no other candidates. The chair of the Education Committee, Sir Offley Wakeman, baronet, was direct and to the point. He looked at me, a young RAF officer aged twenty-five whose total experience of voluntary youth work in Shropshire had been at the Bridgnorth Boys' Club, and bellowed, 'How do you get on with women?' 'Very well Sir,' I replied, but thought it prudent to add that in my RAF work I had given successful talks from time to time to the Wives' Club. The interview was quite short and I was offered the job, which I accepted. I would start on 1st September 1959. My immediate boss would be the County Youth Officer, Jim Knight, who had been a staff officer with Field Marshal

Montgomery as a young brigadier in North Africa and shared his obsession that no report or military appreciation should be longer than one page of foolscap.

The job description was rather broad-brush – to develop youth work in Central Shropshire, an area with one major town, a few declining industrial villages and a lot of countryside. The population of my patch was sixty thousand, the majority in the Borough of Shrewsbury and the rest in the Atcham Rural District which surrounded the town and stretched as far as the Welsh border to the west and south-west. This was one of four youth service areas in the county.

I was required to act as secretary to the Shrewsbury and Atcham Youth Committee. This would be a curious role. I would formally write to the committee with requests and make regular reports. As secretary I would take the minutes and implement committee decisions. This included replying formally to my own letters. The chair was the retired Chief Constable of Shrewsbury, George Macdivitt, a great supporter of our work. He had been chair for many years and for weeks before the annual general meeting people conspired to replace him. Each year they did not have the heart to do so. He always said, 'I am prepared to step down but if you want me to continue I shall be happy to do so.'

My flexibility for action was very wide. The committee met four times a year and tended to rubber stamp everything. There were no planned meetings of the team of four area youth officers. Each of us had autonomy and considerable freedom of action in our own area, peppered with occasional blasts on the telephone from the county youth officer. We found out that this happened every six weeks to all four of us. I think this was a way of giving us a traumatic boost now and again to keep us on our toes.

Before taking up my appointment I had applied for a mortgage and bought my first house in Shrewsbury. I moved my mother to Shrewsbury with me but I soon had to revise these plans. After a year she had another nervous breakdown and was in hospital for six weeks. It was obvious that she needed to be back in her home town and I sold the Shrewsbury house and bought one in Bridgnorth for her. I attempted the forty mile round trip to and from Shrewsbury daily often returning late at night after visits to youth groups. I became physically exhausted and eventually took the six weeks holiday owing to me. I then established a more sensible routine and had a bedsit in Shrewsbury itself and regular time off, returning to Bridgnorth for one night only each week and taking time out for social life. This included drives to Liverpool to visit the pre-Beatles Cavern Club. The regular folk singing stars were Jackie MacDonald and Bridie O'Donnell and we had visiting groups such as The Spinners.

My youth service role had no set boundaries. The nature of youth work itself curtailed my own social life. I did take a girlfriend to Snowdonia on one occasion. On another I called in to see a friend on my way to a rare evening out but noting the engagement ring I did not invite her to join me. The other background pressure was to keep an eye on my mother's health and this sometimes consumed much of my limited free time.

There were no reports of previous youth officer activity because I was the first appointment to the post. The records consisted of an out-of-date address list and nothing else. There were no paid youth workers in the area and all of my contacts would be with a variety of youth groups and uniformed organisations. I made a start by going out to locate the contacts on the list. A few had died and others had handed on their responsibilities but nevertheless this proved to be an excellent way of getting to know my patch. I also spent up to four evenings a week visiting youth clubs. They were very varied in size and clientele but all depended upon voluntary leaders and helpers. There were no local education authority youth centres or paid staff in the clubs in Central Shropshire at that time.

The youth clubs in Shrewsbury were often run by the churches. One, in the centre of town, served young men and women not yet called teenagers who came from a mainly deprived area. The club had a large membership which included some challenging individuals. In this club a short act of worship was required each evening but it was difficult to enforce. In contrast there was a large Methodist youth club with no insistence on church attendance. This club served a slightly more affluent area and young people also met at people's homes. Some of them became regular attenders at the Sunday evening services. Mandatory worship requirements seemed to me to be counterproductive if we were expecting young people to develop as independent young adults.

The village clubs were all led by volunteers at that time generally meeting one evening a week at the village hall. There were some notable exceptions. In the village of Alberbury a couple who were keen on vintage cars and were national joint secretaries of the Riley Register ended up with a youth club that met in the village hall once a week. Club members also 'invaded' their leaders' home every evening. Winter or summer young people would be working in their garage and drinking coffee in their kitchen late into the night. This was the benefit of having highly committed volunteers who gave themselves and their homes fully to the task of working with young people. These contacts with teenagers were invaluable, enabling young people to meet adults in comfortable and friendly surroundings.

The county youth officer had already established weekend residential courses for young people. We found it important to think about course recruitment carefully. A county course with thirty places would soon be full. An area based course for thirty young people also filled up quickly. A course offered to a single youth group would also attract thirty. The closer the offer was to the immediate area the better would be the response, largely because relationships had already been established within the target group. Money was available from county to pay people to lead the courses. For example a jazz course was run one weekend in a hotel on the Welsh border led by Avril Dankworth, sister of Johnny Dankworth. Other special interest courses also provided opportunities to meet people who were leaders in their field.

Outdoor activity courses were run with the help of volunteer instructors. I was able to recruit some excellent activity leaders. One of them, Ken Almond, a technology teacher from a local secondary modern school, helped to lead mountain walking and scrambling courses in Snowdonia. Young people attending the courses were recruited mainly through youth groups but occasionally individuals also applied. Our weekend Snowdonia courses were for groups of twelve young people. There were separate courses for boys and girls in the belief that boys were stronger and faster mountain scramblers, but we never tested out this unfounded assumption. We stayed at the Snowdonia Café in Capel Curig where the owner, Mrs Jones, fed us well and provided a homely atmosphere for the group, although one wet weekend I did see our climbing socks dripping into the bacon frying on the kitchen range. If it was raining at nine o'clock we delayed our start. If rain was still falling at ten, we started, knowing that the weather would generally clear during the day.

We would travel up from Shrewsbury to Capel Curig on the A5 on a Friday evening by minibus. An initial walk on the Saturday was planned on fairly gentle terrain for beginners. The mountain, Meol Siabod, was a favourite. On the Sunday we would tackle something more challenging. This might be Tryfan or the Snowdon Horseshoe. In those days, qualifications such as Mountain Leadership Certificates did not exist, indeed there were no qualification requirements for leaders of expeditions. Vibram soled boots and nylon ropes were just emerging in place of nailed boots and hemp ropes. On one occasion we were accidentally joined by a group of army cadets who appeared suddenly in the mist on Tryfan. They had no leader with them. They had been told to make their way to the summit by their officer. They had no maps or compasses and when we almost collided with them in the mist they were heading in a direction that would have taken them, in two hundred yards, straight over the sheer north face of the mountain. We got them to the top of the mountain then back to lower ground and safety. We did not locate their leader who was highly negligent and had abandoned those cadets, most of them under fifteen, to high risk.

In contrast, two of our young people went for a short walk in a field opposite the Snowdonia Café before breakfast one morning. They were greeted by an approaching man who seemed to have just come down from the mountain top. They noticed he was wearing wellington boots, an item of equipment we banned on the mountain. They politely pointed out to him that he should be wearing climbing boots. He agreed but explained he had only been a short way up the field but that boots should be worn. He then introduced himself as Sir John Hunt of the Everest expedition just out for a pre-breakfast stroll. We were pleased that the training and advice given had been taken to heart by our young climbers.

There were risks in the mountains with new and sometimes challenging situations but the young people generally gained in confidence as they met and overcame their fears. A neighbour of my mother in Bridgnorth asked me to take his fourteen-year-old son on one of our training courses. The boy willingly came along. The most difficult moment was when on the vertiginous knife edge of Crib Goch he had to be roped up and helped along slowly. It took twenty minutes to complete what should have been about a five minute crossing of the ridge. He did make it safely and by the end of the weekend was enthusiastic about his achievement. We learnt some time later that he had become a member of a local climbing club.

I also ran canoe courses some of which were day courses on mainly Grade I water, the easiest. We were fortunate to have easy access to the River Severn which flowed round Shrewsbury but did not quite encircle us. The two river crossings, the English Bridge and the Welsh Bridge, were a reminder of the strategic position of Shrewsbury in the defence and control of the Welsh Marches. A popular Saturday course started at Atcham just downstream of Shrewsbury and ended at Bridgnorth having passed through the Ironbridge Gorge, the cradle of the industrial revolution. An occasional bonus would be the sight of a coracle on the river made by the last coracle maker in this part of England. There were no strict requirements for canoe instructors. The British Canoe Union would eventually establish proper training and controls. The biggest gap in our provision was safety equipment. Two vital protections were yet to be used generally, let alone required, a helmet for climbers and the life jacket and helmet for canoeists.

In the meantime I ran a summer club over a period of six weeks in the large village of Pontesbury, to the south-west of Shrewsbury. I booked the village hall there for one night a week. My youth group members were to be chosen by a piece of social engineering. Every one of twenty or so young men and women in the fourteen to eighteen age range had been recommended by their probation officer. The idea was to offer the usual recreational activities of a youth club in the village hall: coffee bar, table tennis and music, but to work towards a weekend expedition in Snowdonia once the group had practised the appropriate climbing and walking skills.

We had some good hill walking country close to the village on which to practise. On the first evening one of the boys swore at me and left the hall slamming the door. He re-appeared quietly and semi-apologetically the next week. We kept the interest of all twenty young people and I and my voluntary helpers were pleased to work with them. It confirmed what we already knew, that proper preparation of a skill and an opportunity to practise it appeals to many young people and is an important contribution to their social development.

At the end of six weeks we managed a successful weekend in Wales with everyone in the group helping to share duties and working well together as a team. They had learnt new skills and developed some confidence and self-esteem. Long-term success was hard to judge. I met one former tough Shrewsbury youth club member when I revisited the town years later. He was on point duty as a constable with the Shropshire constabulary. He reported that the other hard case was in prison again. He went on to complain about 'young people' but he had to laugh when I reminded him of his own turbulent youth.

There were many voluntary youth workers having success with potentially difficult young people. They were able to influence the young people by means of sharing their own skills and enthusiasm. Near Shrewsbury there was a large village youth club attended by some challenging young people. One evening their voluntary leader announced she was going to see the ballet next week in Birmingham. Fifty club members wanted to go with her by coach and she took them on a trip they greatly enjoyed. Optimism, willingness to extend the boundaries and great expectations of the club members gave her the courage to arrange this unusual and imaginative trip.

The county planned to open a new local educational authority youth centre in the centre of Shrewsbury. A purpose built youth centre would be constructed behind an eighteenth-century town house, Number 5 Belmont. This would become the base for specialist activity groups and clubs for young people in the fourteen to eighteen age range as a shared social hub. A young person would not join the club as a social club but would come along as a member of a specialist group. The entrance through the original front door of 5 Belmont led to a small reception area which had low lights and warm convector heating. The aim was to avoid a threatening searchlight effect for a shy youngster. Beyond this was the well-furnished and decorated coffee bar area. Various rooms and a sports hall offered spaces for groups. If there was any damage such as a broken hook in the cloakrooms it would be repaired by the following morning. Graffiti would be removed straight away. As a result there were rarely any breakages and the young people saw this as their own base and looked after it. Flexible furnishing and rich tapestries were part of the atmosphere. Indeed the quality and warmth of the building were part of our success.

The county youth officer provided detailed advice on organising meetings in the building such as: 'if you have a meeting always put out slightly fewer chairs than you need. When you have to bring out extras people will be encouraged by the better than expected attendance.' The design and high quality of the interior were the inspiration of the county youth officer, Jim Knight. He had no formal training for youth work but his wartime experience in North Africa stood him in good stead. We did not have a motto or corporate aim for the youth service but Jim suggested that if we had one it should be in 'Anglo Saxon', "To cause to bloody well happen!"

Where there were gaps in provision I was given the task of recruiting voluntary youth leaders. It was often difficult to recruit leaders for a general youth club but leaders for specialist groups were easier to get. These people had a passion for their special interests and skills and could not wait to share them with young people. Canoeing, drama, music and judo clubs were quickly started. We established an explorers group whose interests were hiking and climbing. When they reached the age of eighteen the explorers migrated to a newly formed Shrewsbury Mountaineering Club.

The Shrewsbury Youth Centre also provided an ideal base for work with what the youth service used to call 'the unattached'. These were young people not in clubs or organisations and who were seen by many as a social nuisance. One January evening I went to a housing estate in Shrewsbury known for its problem with noisy motorcycles. I met a group of lads and their girls, with the motorcycles under the light of a lamp post. We got into conversation and they said there was nothing to do in Shrewsbury. They would really like a motorcycle club. I said I could help and that we had a place in town where they could meet. I had already approached a former international motorcyclist in the town who had agreed to run the club as a volunteer. At their first meeting with him at Shrewsbury Youth Centre they chose a name for the club: the Grid Club. Activities would include motorcycle maintenance, touring and especially visits to major motorcycle events. One of the tallest young men offered to be honorary treasurer and collected ten shillings a week from each member. Many of them were at work and had money. No one dared to default. Some months later a Girl Guide commissioner was visiting 5 Belmont and flinched when she saw several large, leather jacketed Grid Club members at the entrance. She strode forward bravely and was surprised and pleased to be greeted with a, 'Good evening ma'am.' For once, on neither side did the uniform form a barrier.

The social area did not bring groups together as a single club. People tended to socialise mainly with members of their own specialist group. This specialist group approach brought in young people who would not usually attend a youth club. For example both the judo and explorers clubs drew in members from the Royal Normal College for the Blind when both 'visions' and 'dims' took full part in activities and expeditions. They came all ready with an appetite for challenge. These sixteen- and seventeen-year-olds already cycled at great speed around the quadrangle at their college. The wider community needed to learn that to be visually impaired did not mean that one was socially impaired. Visions and dims, the names used for degree of blindness by the young people themselves, were up for anything. In judo they often had a very keen sense of what the sighted opponent was about to do. One member of the club reached black belt standard relatively quickly.

The most difficult introduction to the Shrewsbury Youth Centre was that of our newly appointed first warden. He was a gifted youth worker and had done well in the National Youth Leaders' Training Course at Leicester but he found the first week daunting. Each evening he did not venture beyond his office. I decided to help him. When he was out early one evening I locked the office and 'lost' the key. This proved to be a miraculous cure and in no time at all he was mixing with the members of the groups and really enjoying his first full-time youth service job. When I returned the key a week later he admitted his 'forced entry' into his new community of young people had been a positive experience and much less scary than he had feared.

Soon the county youth service team expanded. Each area officer was given a full-time assistant which enabled us to expand our work considerably. We did not have funds to pay part-time youth workers but were able to recruit the specialists we needed and could continue to provide training for voluntary leaders when this was not available from one of the National Voluntary Youth Organisations who between them provided good support. My first assistant youth officer, Brian Stock, already had wide experience and would eventually succeed me as area youth officer.

I had become interested in the role of international work camps. The United Nations Work Camps active in Austria were recommended to me by the county youth officer. Plans were made to send twelve young people to Austria to work with refugees and I was to accompany them. We recruited young men and women aged seventeen, some at school and some in employment, to travel to

Austria in August 1961. Potential recruits came with a variety of motivations. All were ready for an adventure, some wanting to help refugees and others ready to seize the opportunity for travel. Eventually the day came when we departed by train to Munich where we would be met and assigned our work camp duties. It was in Munich Railway Station that we received our first shock. The group was split up. Each individual ended up in a different United Nations Association work camp and I was sent as work leader to a camp near Linz, Hitler's intended world capital.

For three weeks the young people worked on a variety of projects. One was in Greece helping a village near the Albanian border develop a drainage system. At night the Albanians would fire rifles over the roofs of the Greek village to remind everyone that they were there. Others worked in different parts of Austria mainly on house building projects. The Linz camp where I ended up was full of Volksdeutch, people of German origin who had been kicked out of Romania when the communists took control. Some families had been in Romania since the thirteenth century but had German names and were therefore evicted. It was our job to help them build their own permanent homes on this hutted camp. Refugees came with a variety of skills. One was an ex-professor of engineering from Bucharest who planned his new house with precision. We were worried about his neighbour, a man whose concrete for the cellar was widening like a fortress because his wooden shuttering was too weak for the concrete. He had also forgotten to provide an entrance door for the cellar, a standard design in Austria. When the problem was pointed out he proposed to get explosives and blow a hole in the new cellar wall. At that point we put him under the close supervision of the former professor of engineering next door.

The workforce was a multinational group of young people. Some were in employment but the majority were students, most of whom were well motivated and worked hard. One less energetic volunteer was the son of an ambassador in Brussels. On my first day I found him sitting down, eating a bag of plums while the rest of the team he was assigned to were working hard shifting bricks. When challenged he said he was a volunteer so he could work when he chose. He was soon re-briefed and sensibly chose to stay and work, otherwise we would have put him on the next train back to Brussels.

When we eventually returned to England each one of the group had enjoyed the experience. For some there were life changing consequences. A young man training to be a chartered surveyor eventually qualified and then sought a job with a community development project in the West Indies. I was convinced that this type of experience would be very valuable for many young people. At that time National Service was just being phased out and a replacement community service programme would have been helpful. Later the USA came up with this idea themselves and I had friends who had participated as volunteers through the work of the Peace Corps. I believe it was a shame that we in Britain did not offer the same universal opportunity for voluntary service to all our young people. It would not have needed to be compulsory but would have attracted large numbers who were looking for adventure and a chance for service to others in need.

One activity we developed in Central Shropshire was the provision of one day 'introduction to work' courses for school leavers. There, fifteen-year-olds in their last year at secondary modern school would soon go on to work or to technical college. We provided day courses and recruited a team of volunteers to lead them. The topics included money management, and we provided careers advice.

Another aspect of our work was the area round of County Youth Drama and Public Speaking competitions. The drama festival made it possible for young people to perform in public and some were also recruited to help organise the competition itself. For example I had one keen and effective stage manager aged seventeen who aspired to a career in theatre management. At this time these youth service activities were providing useful extensions to the voluntary extra-curricular work being undertaken in some of the secondary modern and grammar schools in Shrewsbury.

The LEA (Local Education Authority) youth service in Shropshire was run by a small team of youth officers who sought to tap the voluntary efforts of adult and young people. Gradually youth work was to become more and more professionalised. My five years as youth officer for Central Shropshire provided excellent experience and enabled me to develop my ideas about work with young people. Over time there was an increase in the number of professional youth workers. As their numbers increased it was important to retain and if possible grow the number of adults who were prepared to volunteer and share their special interests and expertise with young people. Special interest groups were a more intensive and realistic means of engaging with young people than providing only social venues where leaders had to work hard to make their club more than just 'somewhere to go'. Those clubs that were started by churches to influence young people seemed to have greater success when elements of compulsion were not part of the ethos.

In terms of youth service building design, the Shrewsbury Youth Centre initiative demonstrated to me that if you provide high quality facilities young people will appreciate them especially where as a member of a group they see them as their home base for social activities.

An important deficiency was the absence of the training needed by volunteer youth workers, particularly in high risk areas such a canoeing and mountain scrambling. I was fortunate to find activity leaders with the relevant skills and experience.

The experience of the work camps in Austria fulfilled a need to engage young people in voluntary service. They were helping to alleviate real problems for others and experienced 'growth' in their own lives. Voluntary service was a means of personal growth and for a few a life-changing experience

During my five years in the Shropshire youth services the school system in Shrewsbury was selective. Shrewsbury itself had a Junior Technical High School. The 1944 Education Act allowed for their development. The task of the youth service was to ensure that everyone would learn how to use their leisure well in a world which would soon have full employment and shorter working hours. This belief underpinned our work in the youth service. Continuing education was considered to be the way forward including lifelong learning. This vision would not be sustained as in the coming years other high profile political ideas dominated the direction of comprehensive schooling: removal of surplus school places, stimulation of parent influence and 'choice' of school and later clearly targeted attempts to 'raise standards' a general term that became restricted to academic standards all measured by tests and examination. The focus would move away from education for leisure. In 1959 the youth service was still seen as an important part of our education services aimed at developing the whole person, lifelong.

After five years in Shropshire I began to look for another challenge in informal education. My applications were for jobs in youth work. One job offered an opportunity to work with young people in Kenya; another a chance to train youth workers in three local education authorities, Devon, Exeter and Plymouth.

The first reply to my applications came from Devon and I was invited to interview at County Hall, Exeter. On my way from the railway station to County Hall I passed a prominent poster outside a church exhorting me like Joshua, to 'be strong and of a good courage'. This cheered me on my way. The County Hall building proved to be less prominent. Apparently, when it was built the height of its clock tower was reduced by the Exeter City Council. They did not want an unduly prominent county building on their patch.

I went to the interview and was offered the job. The task was to train full-time and part-time professional youth workers in the County of Devon, the City of Exeter and the

City of Plymouth. My paymasters would be Devon County Council. Later, the county borough of Torbay would be established and I would be working for four local education authorities. I thought it was very generous of Devon to do all the spadework for the other LEAs. I soon found out why. In a year's time the Devon county youth officer, Bob Hook, a former international rugby player, was retiring. My job description would then expand to encompass the role of county youth officer for Devon in addition to my multi-authority training role. This seemed like a very challenging prospect but I would have about nine months to work alongside Bob. We were being paid on the same salary grade. The arrangement worked well. Bob was looking forward to retirement and I was eager to get going on my new job. Bob enabled me to get established in my Devon role very quickly.

The Devon LEA had an excellent residential training centre on Dartmoor which provided facilities for schools and youth organisations. There were four area youth officers in Devon, one of whom became youth officer for Torbay when the new authority was established. I also worked with the city youth officer in Exeter and the youth officer for the City of Plymouth. I was fortunate in that hotels in Torquay and Teignmouth were available at low cost in the winter as bases for residential courses. Much youth leader training took place in those hotels. They accommodated day courses as well as residential weekends. I also had a wider training role in that I organised a south west youth leader training course that served all the south west LEAs and was based in Gloucestershire. The dominant workforce in youth clubs was voluntary and the training provided an opportunity for volunteers to meet voluntary youth workers throughout the south west.

When I took over as the Devon County Youth Officer in April 1966, I added some interesting jobs to my CV. For example I was responsible for administering grants to youth organisations in Devon. Most of these applications were straightforward but there were occasional exceptions. One day I received a request for a grant to buy a table tennis table. This came from the Dartmouth Boys' Club. We had not seen anything about its activities for years so I thought it necessary to go and visit the club to see for myself what it was doing. On a dark autumn evening I drove to Dartmouth. The club building was lit up and the club was in session. There were about twelve boys present. The membership was probably unique in youth service history, all of the boys appeared to be over sixty years of age. These were all long-standing members of the club. Unfortunately our grants were for members in the fourteen to twenty age range. An application during the 1920s might have been successful.

As county youth officer I was attending county council committees from time to time. I had come to know Devon very well. On my first morning a colleague had driven me across Dartmoor on a visit to a youth officer and I became aware of the beauty and size of the county.

Once I assumed my full role my immediate boss Brian Laister, an assistant education officer, and I discussed the need for schools to play their part in providing support to young people in their leisure time. I began to consider and explore current community schools' initiatives in England.

In several authorities full-time teaching posts had been established, half the time was to be teaching and the other half was to run a youth club on school premises. The inevitable happened. Both teaching and youth work demand extra hours and energy to succeed and such posts, with conflicting demands and sometimes two bosses, proved to be difficult. I also looked at other options, in particular at early experiments in using schools as a major resource for the community. Examples included the development of Village Colleges in Cambridgeshire and the community role of the High Schools in Leicestershire. It was obvious that to do anything significant this would have to be a full-time supernumerary post with only a small teaching load. I soon realised that a school would need a youth tutor with a small timetable to help the tutor to get to know the young people. The youth tutor would be fully on the school staff, and school governors would have to agree that youth work was a key part of the school's service to the community. The school itself would provide a base and resources for young people but, in a large rural county, schools could also offer help and support to surrounding volunteer-run youth and community groups.

The Education Committee agreed to establish an informal working party. Membership included three secondary school head teachers, an area youth officer, a head of further education at a technical college, the warden of the Further Education Centre at Dartington Hall, a lecturer from Rolle College of Education, the director of religious education in the Exeter Diocese, the director of the community Council of Devon, an HMI (Her Majesty's Inspector), my immediate boss, Brain Laister, a senior education officer and myself.

I was secretary and the group was chaired by John Gale, headmaster of Ilfracombe Grammar School.

We reported in 1966. Our report 'the Development of Community Colleges' examined the advantages of using school facilities for supporting work with the local community. This included community developments based on school premises. The Education Committee adopted the report and the detailed administrative arrangements in the appendices and agreed to establish the Devon Community College policy. As a result, a group of schools volunteered to pilot our suggested developments and youth tutors were appointed. On the basis of the good work done by the pilot schools, other schools asked to have Community College status as well. The use of willing volunteers for the pilot project worked well. Other schools and their communities had an opportunity to see the early successes.

Such developments required careful preliminary work. There was one secondary school in the north of the county where the governors, while not being resistant to change, wanted time to consider new initiatives carefully. The chair of governors put it this way: 'Come back and tell us about it again.' This was not an obstructive move but a recognition that careful consideration was required. When that governing body decided to proceed they committed themselves fully to the promotion of community work.

On arrival in Devon I had become a regular boarder at the Glendale Hotel in Exeter. After long hours as a youth officer in Central Shropshire my more strategic role in Devon gave me evenings off to redevelop my social life. Exeter offered plenty of relaxation. Just down the road from the Glendale was the Jolly Porter pub which was the venue for weekly meetings of the Exeter Folk Club. Devon offered the delights of the sea and the moor. There were always invitations to other events. The hospital events were popular. They offered meetings with staff and punches which seemed strong enough to contain surgical spirit, and apparently some of them did.

Soon after I arrived in Devon I met a girl who was a laboratory technician at the Royal Devon and Exeter Hospital. One Sunday afternoon I took her in my relatively new lease car, a Ford Cortina, on a Royal Devon and Exeter Hospital treasure hunt. We negotiated many roads and a few bumpy country lanes. In the back seat was my old university friend from Leeds, Nick Hodges, who had come down to Devon to run the Babychick clothing factory in Tiverton. With him was another young laboratory technician. Within a month I had been dumped by my girlfriend for a Devon policeman and my future wife, Gill, had dropped the man from Babychick. Within months I had proposed and was accepted over a cup of cocoa at the Glendale Hotel where I lodged.

We were married in Tawstock Parish Church near Barnstaple in September 1966 and established our first home together in Exminster near Exeter. We quickly acquired a basset hound, a wedding present with an insatiable hound appetite and thieving skills. In October 1967 our first child Richard (Dik) was born at home. I remember a nerve wracking train journey to and from York where I was to address a national youth service conference, when Gill was two weeks overdue. There were no mobile telephones and I had to use call boxes at stations en route to check on the situation at home. Luckily I arrived back in good time for a successful home delivery a week later.

In view of my much increased responsibilities my immediate boss suggested that I apply for a pay rise. I did this but it was turned down by the Education Committee. I was happy in Devon with a newish job, new friends and especially a new wife and family, however, in the spring of 1969 I saw an advertisement for a new post in Somerset. It was for an assistant education officer (AEO) youth. This had been created by the recently appointed chief education Officer, Robert Parker. He had just come from West Sussex where he had been instrumental in creating an AEO youth post. I prepared an application and approached my referees. One of them the county youth officer for Shropshire was willing to give me a reference but he warned me that Parker was a hard man. Apparently he was well-known for sacking people as a regular personnel practice. He took no prisoners. I ignored the advice having worked with a hard man before, namely this particular referee. I applied for the post, was shortlisted and travelled to Taunton for interview. I was offered the post by Robert Parker and accepted. I knew that my wide and growing responsibilities and experiences had prepared me well for promotion. I only learnt when I started in Somerset that my referee from Shropshire had intended to apply for the job himself. I can only assume that he had reconsidered his position and had left the field open for me.

The Devon County LEA had provided me with experience in many aspects of educational administration and management. I had been given considerable freedom in my role, which had also allowed me to practise my public speaking skills beyond Devon. I began to speak at education conferences and was able to gain a broader view of youth and community services in England and Wales.

In Devon I was also able to pursue my own leisure interests. With a teacher from Teignmouth Grammar School I was able to bring about the establishment of the South West Orienteering Association. This was a sport I had already encountered and developed in Shropshire. Dartmoor was a wonderful place for adventure and I also served as a Duke of Edinburgh Award expedition assessor on Dartmoor. Gill and I were building our family and saw quite a bit of her parents who, on one occasion, looked after Richard and also our wayward basset hound when we took a holiday with friends in the Scilly Isles. When we moved to Somerset it was a wrench to leave Devon. Gill had grown up in Devon at Woolacombe and had subsequently moved to Exeter. Our first child, Richard, was born in Devon and we had Gill's parents living near Moretonhampstead on Dartmoor.

This would become a standard pattern. The family moved to meet my career aspirations. Once I left Devon, my successor, the former youth officer for the Inner London Education Authority, secured my job and also the pay rise I had been refused. In turn I was about to succeed a county youth officer whose job had been abolished on his retirement. I was about to enter the magic circle of education administrators.

5

local government – at work and play

I n July 1969 I started work in Somerset. I was now a third tier education administrator reporting to a sub-committee of the Education Committee. My role had expanded rapidly as had education administration itself. It is important to realise that in the 1960s the counties I worked for did not have highly politicised county councils and service expansion was largely officer led. The service grew and changed radically as I moved from Shropshire to Devon and then Somerset and Lincolnshire.

In Shropshire I had encountered and observed from afar someone who had been appointed secretary for education in the 1930s. This was H Martin Wilson who was a remote figure. After meeting him at my appointment to the post of youth officer for Central Shropshire I never met him again. He had begun to develop an education department in Shrewsbury but he never adopted the title of chief education officer. His title was secretary for education. I saw him only from a distance. When I left Shrewsbury Youth Centre late at night I often saw the light on in his office. This confirmed the generally accepted view that he often worked long into the night. I also heard that each day at noon he would send his secretary out to bring him a light lunch which included a handful of currants. He would then change into his dressing gown and take a nap in the office. He would give strict instructions not to be disturbed until a specific time. Sometimes this was to enable him to catch a train to London.

As stated already, my occasional communications with Jim Knight the county youth officer were by telephone. I never rang him. He rang me mainly to deliver the six-weekly youth officer team rocket. The only other administrator I met was a young education administrator, John Tomlinson. I met him when I sought six weeks' leave to recover from exhaustion following my visit to workcamps in Europe. He was clearly probing to find out if the county youth officer was a slave driver. I did not let on about the management style of my immediate boss because I felt he did an excellent job as a dynamic leader of some exciting developments in the county. John Tomlinson probably suspected that we were under pressure from time to time. This is the only conversation I had with him. John would go on to become director of education in Cheshire.

The education department in Shropshire was at an early stage of development with a lean administration and a seemingly apolitical county council. Not long after I left

Shropshire Martin Wilson retired. In retirement he went to Chile to reform the education service for President Allende. I met a Chilean educator years later on a visit he made to the Somerset LEA. He declared Martin Wilson to be very clever but 'a very hard man'.

My move to Devon was a move to a well-developed education administration. The concept of corporate management had not yet arrived. I became part of a large professional department complete with chief education officer, several education officers, a chief inspector, a large team of advisers and a large administrative workforce. In Devon I was outside the loop in terms of providing a service directly to a county committee.

Chief executives had not been invented. Instead the county clerk provided a legal service to the Devon County Council and its committees. He had an unusual initiation ceremony for new lawyers joining his staff. He used to take them for a grand tour of Devon and drop them home well fed and 'watered'. I visited him once and was offered a drink from a carafe of clear liquid on his desk. I declined having heard that it contained strong gin and tonic.

In Somerset I was now fully integrated into the education department structure with a committee responsibility. The officer hierarchy was typical. At this time many education officers were Oxbridge graduates. We had the chief education officer, the deputy chief education officer, two senior education officers and myself and three other assistant education officers with specific areas of responsibility. Below us were the chief clerk, section heads and other administrators and clerks. These were mainly local people who had attended the grammar schools or independent schools in the area. They had not gone to university but like many able students in a county town they had chosen to join a highly respected local government administration where they would be guaranteed a lifelong career. They had considerable knowledge of the education service in Somerset and were the heart of the administrative machine. As in Devon there was not yet a chief executive, that innovation would come later after local government reorganisation.

The elected county councillors in Somerset described themselves as independents. Many did have political affiliations but, in 1969, Somerset did not have political divisions or party groups in the governance of the county. There was one county councillor who was overtly a member of the Labour Party. This was Stephen Morland, a notable Somerset businessman. He was always elected by the other councillors as chair of the Education Committee because they thought he was doing the job well. County councillors at this time did not get paid but were volunteers who only received travel expenses.

I commuted to Somerset daily for several months because we were unable to sell our house in Devon. Eventually we were able to rent the schoolhouse at the South Somerset hamstone village of Hinton St George. The school was still operational but the head teacher preferred to live in her own house in a nearby village. We rented from January 1970 because my wife Gill was due to give birth to our second child, Katherine, in the April and we had to make a move before the sale of our Devon house was completed.

I have described the administrative structure in Somerset. My immediate boss was Roger Bull, the senior education officer responsible for further education. However Chief Education Officer Robert Parker had other ideas. He tended to go directly to people if he wanted information or wished to give them a task. As he had a special interest in my area of responsibility, the youth service, this happened to me quite frequently. When I arrived in July 1969 he told me there were two priorities, one was to sort out the current youth service staffing and the other was to find a sailing base for a small fleet of six-berth sailing cruisers to be used by Somerset schools. Sailing was his passion. He would work long days and most evenings from Mondays to Fridays and would go off to sail from the Isle of Wight at weekends.

I moved quickly to get to know my new county. We had a residential youth centre based in an old manor house at Kilve on the North Somerset coast. I visited on a fine summer morning. It was known that Bob Parker had recently remarried following a divorce. The Kilve Court groundsman met me and showed me round. He suddenly blurted out, 'I see that the chief education officer has been fined for adultery.' I carefully explained that a divorce settlement had been reached and he had now remarried.

Kilve had a dynamic warden who provided a base for a wide range of outdoor activities and cultural and other courses for young people from schools and youth organisations in Somerset. We were fortunate to have several residential centres in the county. Somerset also had a residential adult education centre at Dillington House, once the home of Lord North who lost us the American colonies. We also had other camp sites and field centres and an astronomical telescope on the Mendips.

The Somerset Youth Service had some fifty full-time staff of area youth officers and youth club leaders. There were some problems to address, particularly the work pressure for some of the leaders who were required to run a youth club half of the time and also teach half of the time in a secondary school. We introduced youth tutor posts on the Devon model and made some club leaders into senior leaders who were given a youth service training and a supervisory role.

I spent a lot of time looking for a sailing base in Dorset, a good opportunity to get to know the Dorset coast. I found nothing suitable or available in Poole Harbour itself but I found a base at Ridge Wharf on the River Frome at Wareham, which for several years was used by Somerset schools. I put in a lot of driving out of county and was properly authorised to do so. In contrast one of my youth officers, Major Gus Moore, was challenged when he travelled through Dorset for two or three miles on his way to Henstridge which was a Somerset outpost. The chief clerk of the education department refused his travel claim because it was unauthorised for an out of county visit. Gus appealed to the chief education officer who ruled in his favour. Had Gus tried to drive strictly within Somerset it would have involved a diversion of some ten miles. Bob Parker was good at cutting red tape and I never found him a difficult person to work with; he would allow mistakes as long as they were different each time. If you went to him with a problem you also had to recommend a solution and invariably he agreed to my suggestions even though he always said, 'I am prepared to listen to you with a closed mind.'

I had the new experience of advising an education sub-committee. The chair was Marjorie Hickling, a Conservative county councillor who had attempted once to become a parliamentary candidate in order to unseat the Labour Member of Parliament for Cannock. She had gone down the coal mines to talk to the miners direct. The Labour member held on but she reduced his majority. With a chair like this, and the chief education officer's interest in youth work, we were about to experience a sudden explosion of youth provision. I had briefed Marjorie about our need to reorganise and expand our staffing in youth clubs and schools. My plans were passed by the Youth sub-committee. Not wanting to waste time Marjorie put a special motion to the quarterly meeting of the full council. She explained that we only spent 0.4% of the county budget on the youth service. We actually had quite a large budget by youth service standards at the time but when she described our seemingly niggardly share of county council funds there were gasps of horror and possibly a cry of 'shame'. In one well-timed strike at full council we had our youth service budget doubled.

There was now a busy period implementing the proposed developments. One morning in the summer of 1971 the chief clerk of the education department met me in the corridor and said, 'the boss wants to know if you would like to go on this.' He handed me a brochure from the Henley Management College, Greenlands. This college ran regular general management courses for senior managers in the private and public sectors. The course would be for three months from January to March 1972. I would also attend a basic accounts and statistics course at the college beforehand. It was an attractive offer because all my fees would be paid and I would continue to receive my salary while at Henley. By now we had sold our house in Exeter and got to know local friends through the church and also through the playgroup. I decided to accept the nomination and was selected for course Session 75. There was one immediate downside. We were not allowed home for the first three weekends and that would be the first separation since our marriage. In addition, the schoolhouse had other residents and Gill often heard the mice scuttling about behind the wainscot although they never dared to appear, possibly for fear of the basset hound.

The Henley course was attended by sixty-five senior managers from private and public enterprises. All were men. We were divided into seminar groups called syndicates. I was in a group of ten which included myself, from local government, a banker, a civil servant, an army officer, an insurance manager (his area was Africa and Asia), three from manufacturing industries, and three others representing the Bahamas Electricity Corp, a gas board and the UK Atomic Energy Authority.

The syndicate method of teaching was a successful learning strategy, effectively covering extensive reading material and producing reports in a relatively short time. Each individual had sole responsibility to feed back to the group on specific reading sources. There were plenary speakers, outside visits and syndicate discussions. We also had specific seminars on financial management, analytical methods and economics. The only weak aspect was marketing. A leading professor of marketing gave us a lecture using a specific company as an example of best marketing practice. Unfortunately the next day its problems with an aircraft engine featured as the big news story nationally.

I found the Henley course immensely helpful enabling the development of my understanding of management outside the local government and education context. The students learnt from each other and personality tests helped us understand ourselves and highlighted our management styles. Three of us who had shown a creative personality profile were planted in groups which had been given the task of managing a challenge to create a profit for their company. We were all from the public sector or banking and it was interesting that those project groups with creative plants yielded the best financial results.

On my return to the office at the end of March I was immediately seen by Bob Parker, the chief education officer, who gave me a great surprise by offering me a sideways move from youth service to the post of assistant education officer for sites and buildings. This would involve running the whole of the education capital building programme for the larger pre local government, reorganisation of Somerset stretching from Exmoor to the boundaries of Bristol and Bath. He asked if I would accept the transfer at once but I said I would like to consider the offer overnight. He joked that Henley had slowed up my response time. Next morning I accepted and was excited to think about the challenge of handling a fast-growing building programme for schools and further education (FE) colleges. Henley had proved to be a great experience. It also became the gateway to a wider responsibility and what was now to become a career in education administration.

My sideways move took me round the corridor and into an office slightly nearer to the Deputy Chief Education Officer, George Rankin. George, who had also served as deputy to Bob Parker's predecessor, was a gentle and cultured man. He had presided over many developments. Somerset had decided in the 1950s to introduce comprehensive schools gradually as circumstances and funds allowed. Changes were made on education grounds and in careful consultation with the public. Several secondary comprehensive schools with an eleven to eighteen age range had been developed by 1970. Many of these were in the north of the county in the fast-growing population areas which served the commuters of Bristol, Bath and Weston-super-Mare. George was also about to develop a comprehensive system on Exmoor where middle schools in Williton, Dulverton and Minehead sent pupils of thirteen to eighteen to the upper school in Minehead on the former grammar school site. This avoided long rural journeys for eleven-year-olds. In the 1960s, Somerset had also closed about one hundred small primary schools, although there were still two hundred and fifty primaries with some small rural schools surviving. The ones in West Somerset now had a new role as first schools transferring pupils to the middle schools at Dulverton, Minehead and Williton.

I was also responsible for further education college and youth service building projects in liaison with my previous boss, Roger Bull, the senior education officer for Further education. Robert Parker continued his usual practice of consulting more junior staff directly so in some ways I was responsible to three senior colleagues. Robert Parker was the supremo and from time to time the words on the telephone 'come in' quickly propelled any one of us into his presence.

My first long journey with George Rankin was to a meeting of the south west branch of the Society of Education Officers. The meeting was in Winchester. George allowed two hours for the journey and we arrived very early. This gave us time to look around the Peter Simmonds Sixth Form College where we were to meet. George introduced me to several colleagues. This was the beginning of a long and happy membership of this professional organisation. After a while I became secretary of the south west region.

The pressure to reorganise schools had now escalated with a requirement on LEAs to implement comprehensive schemes. Things were also developing politically at local level and the chairman of the Schools Sub-committee, an active Conservative councillor, was proactive in pressing for reorganisation. His preference was for middle schools.

The development of comprehensive schemes was influenced by what might be the flavour of the year. The original schemes had favoured a system of eleven to eighteen age-range comprehensive schools. This model was used for the very first comprehensives in the county. The next favoured solution was the middle school which was promoted for educational reasons. Middle schools, for the nine to thirteen age-range, were established not only in West Somerset but also the Cheddar Valley and the Ilminster/Crewkerne area in the south of the county. The next favoured idea was to establish eleven to sixteen age-range comprehensive schools leading to a sixth form college. That was a preferred solution when George and I attended my first SEO meeting in Winchester. Hampshire had implemented a sixth form college model across the county.

Another preffered option arrived in Somerset following a visit to Sweden by Robert Parker. Sweden had a tertiary college system. All students went on at sixteen to a tertiary college. In this model eleven to sixteen age-range comprehensives would lead into a college which included all technical, professional and academic courses for young people at sixteen. In the Swedish model there were twenty-two lines of post-sixteen study open to young people. Somerset would go on to develop tertiary college systems in the Bridgwater, Yeovil and Street areas, and later, a sixth form college at Taunton.

Meanwhile Somerset was awarded an Organisation for Economic Co-operation and Development (OECD) accolade for the design of a new eleven to eighteen age-range comprehensive school at Worle near West-super-Mare. I helped to welcome our international visitors who admired aspects such as the central library and resource area. A year after when the school was in session I noted that subject departments held onto their own resources. The new internationally acclaimed central resource area was mainly used as a spare classroom. It is good to design an up-to-date comprehensive school but I realised that the full benefits of a new school building are not achieved until the teachers are also updated and gain ownership of the ideas that inspired the original design. The best way was to involve teachers fully in the production of the design brief for the school and to provide relevant training through that process. The other discovery was that it was always better to plan pathways after the pupils had used a new building for a while. Pathways could then follow the best routes naturally trodden by their feet.

I was enjoying my job when local government reorganisation changed the map of Somerset in 1974; at a stroke we lost a third of the county to the new County of Avon. Robert Parker and some other long-serving officers retired and the rest of us had to apply for jobs in the new Somerset under a new chief education officer, Barry Taylor. The county council changed its staffing structure and appointed a new chief executive. County councillors changed too. They were now selected by their party groups and would develop a political structure. For a while committee structures remained unchanged but the controlling group would seek a majority on all committees.

In the summer of 1973 Gill and I and our three children, Richard, Katherine and Andrew who was now six months old, had enjoyed a low budget camping holiday in Brittany with friends. On our return I began the task of considering my place in the new structure. Somerset was about to lose a third of its territory and population to the new County of Avon. The major part of the building programmes I had been dealing with was to go with them. My choice was either to work for Somerset or move to Bristol. As a family we wanted to stay in Somerset and our home at Hinton St George.

The new chief education officer for Somerset had established a flatter staffing structure for the new education department. There would be four deputy chief education officer posts of equal status with assistant education officers below them. I applied for a deputy chief education officer post and was delighted to be appointed as deputy chief education officer for further education. I held the post for six weeks. Then my new boss, Barry Taylor, called me in and asked me to take the post of deputy chief education officer for administration. I accepted. The title seemed boring and restrictive but the job description gave me wide responsibilities within the education department and the job turned out to be much more exciting than the title implied. I was to be responsible for the education department budget, its staff and all building programmes. There was another major role which arose from the county council's new structure, I was to be responsible for links with the chief executive and the other county council departments. The post was my entry ticket into the new world of corporate management.

The new Somerset County Council had been elected for the first time on party political tickets. One or two independents survived, one of whom was correctly able to describe his day job as 'of independent means'. The independent was now an endangered species, however. There was a Conservative majority which included many experienced former 'independent' councillors.

The first task of the new council was to appoint the county's first chief executive, Maurice Gaffney. He had been chief executive of a water authority and had also held other senior positions in the private sector. The expectation was that he would weld the new county council into a single effective business serving the people of Somerset. His first move was to prepare a corporate plan for the whole county council. He asked each department to appoint a deputy to serve on a corporate management group which would bring this change about.

The chief education officer nominated me to represent the education department. In one stroke of the pen I found myself in a group which the chief executive deemed to be the real management board of the Somerset County Council. Deputies from other major departments, social services, transport and treasurers departments had also been nominated to join the group. Maurice Gaffney was well focused and open to ideas. The problem was that the departmental chief officers were conscious of their sector's statutory responsibilities and this did not align with Maurice's view of corporate management at all. Chief officers' concerns spread to the elected councillors. They had wanted a smack of firm government and some military drive and effectiveness to create change. The elected members quickly realised that although the post of chief executive was needed, they did not need the accompanying hassle and an implied reduction in their chief officers' departmental management or political control if they were confined to the strategic task of a board of directors. Within six months even the leading county councillor who had appointed Maurice thought it time for a change and he was 'offered' immediate early retirement. This was good news for chief officers of departments who had seen a great threat to their autonomy.

This experience gave an excellent overview of the county council and its activities. It also helped me to develop ideas about reorganisation of large and complex management structures. There had been no real consideration of the existing roles and responsibilities of chief officers and the duties assigned to them by statute. Nor had there been any appreciation of the danger that a chief executive officer might inadvertently cut across the duties and obligations of elected members and the county council committees. Maurice Gaffney's successor was the serving county treasurer who worked well and cooperatively with his fellow chief officers including his successor, the new county treasurer. Officers and elected members gave a corporate sigh of relief but ditched the corporate plan and its working party.

My responsibility for the education budget gave me an opportunity for informal meetings with civil servants. Once a quarter, an undersecretary from the Department of Education and Science (DES) came down with a colleague to Dillington House, our residential adult education college. Our Chief Education Officer, Barry Taylor, and I attended together with a colleague from the county treasurer's department who handled the education budget. The name of our group was the Programme Budgeting Club. We had wide ranging discussions on the development of education funding nationally. Lunch was provided and on occasion our London visitors stayed on for a game of croquet.

After four years in the job a colleague retired and I was invited, in 1979, to move sideways to take over the role of deputy chief education officer, schools, getting fully involved in all aspects including school reorganisation and the completion of a move to some form of comprehensive reorganisation throughout Somerset. The comprehensive school map of Somerset was a patchwork, influenced by the change of favoured solutions over time. We had all of the historical flavours of the month: eleven to eighteen age-range comprehensives; three areas with nine to twelve middle schools and thirteen to eighteen upper schools, and three tertiary college areas with eleven to sixteen secondary schools.

There were two areas which ended up with hybrid solutions. The Taunton area had four eleven to sixteen age-range schools. One of these was a joint Anglican and Roman Catholic Voluntary Aided Comprehensive School. I had the pleasure of selling to the church authorities an LEA secondary school building and playing fields which they purchased with the help of a ninety per cent central government grant. In Taunton we established a sixth form college on the site of the former boys' grammar school but the FE college remained separate.

The Bruton area was also complex and, as a training task, new administrative assistants in the education department would be given the thankless job of trying to produce a paper recommending a comprehensive school system for the area. There were secondary modern schools at Wincanton, Ansford and Bruton and a boys' grammar school (Sexey's School) with a boarding facility. Girls' grammar school places were bought in at Sunnyhill, an independent girls' school in Bruton.

Eventually a scheme was agreed. This made Sexey's School co-educational and comprehensive. Its sixth form also served students from the two eleven to sixteen age-range comprehensive schools at Ansford and Wincanton. Sexey's School continued to provide boarding places as well. Sexey was a seventeenth-century benefactor but the name created a number of funny stories, some true. An elderly ex-pupil of Sexey's boys' school had been to a reunion. After the event he drove his Jaguar car down the hill to Bruton town centre. On the way he saw a group of girls from Sunnyhill School walking in the rain and stopped. He wound down his window and said, 'Would you like a lift. I'm a Sexey old boy.' Apparently they ran away in terror.

I assumed the role of first deputy in 1979, as our dynamic Chief Education Officer Barry Taylor was increasingly being involved in national and international education activities. At one point in the early 1980s, the controlling party group considered rationalising schooling provision on Exmoor. The proposal was to turn Dulverton First School into a full primary school, close the very small Dulverton Middle School and transfer pupils at eleven to the Upper School at Minehead which would become an eleven to eighteen age-range comprehensive. The chair of the Education Committee, Lt Col Tony Dowse Brennan, a former army education officer, and I set off for a protest meeting at Dulverton Middle School on Exmoor. We both had severe reservations about the plan but, like me, he was delegated to go and face the music. This we did in a packed Dulverton Middle School hall. We had two hours of protest which did not quite get as far as physical violence. We left with the clear message that Dulverton would oppose the plan as a community by every possible means short of lynching. On the way out of the school car park the chair turned to me and said, 'I don't think we'll bother, do you?' We easily persuaded the party group leader and the chief education officer to drop the whole idea. It would have faced great opposition and would have increased building and transport costs as well as disrupting a popular middle school system.

The new Somerset suffered from the loss of long-serving administrative officers in 1974. Being highly able administrators, they took the offer of early retirement speedily. They also took with them a great deal of information about the education service and left a yawning gap in the advice given to elected members and senior officers. One who retired in 1974 was Len Allen, the principal administrative officer for sites and buildings. On his last day he unlocked a desk drawer and handed me a letter from the Department of Education and Science (DES). This he had used to win us many approvals for capital projects over the years. We had attributed his success to his power of eloquence. I am sure that his skills of persuasion helped but the letter from the DES was his secret weapon as it conceded a point of principle and was always the silver bullet that brought success. He handed it over with the solemnity of an Isaiah handing over his mantle to the next prophet. Other senior education officer colleagues who had joined the county council from school had detailed knowledge of Somerset schools including the availability of extra land and the dynamics of the local scene that would ensure successful negotiations for school building projects. Much of this information was not on file but in the heads of education administrators and was lost to the department on their retirement. In time we built up our own background knowledge but we could not rival the experience of administrators who had worked on constant reorganisations, building programmes and school closures over four decades.

Due to the chief education officer's national and international education initiatives, as first deputy, I had good experience of running an education service. Barry Taylor's management style encouraged people to develop in their roles and was always supportive. He proved a training ground for leadership. Four deputies were appointed in 1974. One, who was later designated first deputy, retired in 1979. The other three of us ended up as chief education officers in Stockport, Essex and Lincolnshire.

Barry encouraged us to widen our experience beyond Somerset. In 1980, I was offered the first Association of Education Committees Bursary to look at head teacher training in Europe, and after completing my study I was asked almost immediately to address conferences in Windsor and later Milan. I was a little sceptical about being called an expert on the strength of six months travelling around in Europe. This and other experiences are described in later chapters.

6

---

the audit commission and other 'excursions'

I n 1981, I was one of two education officers seconded to the Audit Commission to advise on their study of non-teaching costs in secondary schools. The commission itself was a newly established body. Its controller was John Banham. The other education officer seconded for this study was Chris Tipple, director of education in Northumberland. Subsequently our appointment was announced by *The Times Educational Supplement* on 18th May 1984 thus: 'Just in case the city gents from Deloitte didn't appreciate the delicate relationship between caretakers and the teaching process, the commission arranged for the secondment of a couple of LEA bureaucrats... to assist them with this gap in their adult education.' We worked alongside a team from Deloitte Haskins and Sells.

The study had been established to look at value for money in secondary schools. At that time, in an education spend on secondary education of £3.7 billion, £1.25 billion was being spent on non-teaching staff, premises, supplies and transport. We were to provide an audit guide following fieldwork in twelve local education authorities, looking at a sample of secondary schools within each one. In the fieldwork I was teamed up with Leila Fanous, who had banking experience and knowledge of independent school budgets. In an article for *Education* magazine in May 1984, I recorded my impressions at the time. There was a general willingness by head teachers and education officers to seek more effective ways of managing the service. Pressures on local education authorities and schools were exacerbated by sudden decisions to freeze staff vacancies. Such policies to achieve short term economies could be at the cost of efficiency and effectiveness. Even within this group of twelve LEAs there were great variations in the funds available for education, straining relationships between education officers and schools.

I found the definitions used by the Audit Commission very helpful in terms of reviewing budgets. The 'three Es' of economy, efficiency and effectiveness were all to be examined in any urgent reviews. Economy could not be allowed to create inefficiencies or damage the effectiveness of the service provided to the public. The study made a significant case for the delegation of budgets to schools. The Audit Commission experience proved invaluable later for my implementation of a scheme in Lincolnshire. My own education was not confined to the boundaries of my professional life. Continuing education, lifelong education, informal education and community education are terms that recognise the wider context in which we learn. We talk about learning for life when the whole of life is learning. Since 1970, our family life had been focused on the village of Hinton St George in Somerset. When I moved to work in the Somerset education department we rented the schoolhouse at Hinton as a temporary measure until our Devon house was sold. For a period of six years we were drawn into the permanent life of the village and eventually bought a cottage in West Street, moving house with the help of several friends and the pub beer trolley.

The Earl Poulett had retired to Jersey in 1959. When we arrived many of the people who had worked on the estate had been given a chance to buy their cottages. Hinton House, the home of the Earl was derelict. The school and schoolhouse were in a building in West Street which ended in the former kitchen garden of the big house. There was also what looked like a bombed site in West Street where the George and Crown pub had burnt to the ground some years earlier. There was another pub in the High Street called the Poulett Arms. In our first week I called in late one evening for a pint and was told: 'it's nearly closing time. I'll give you half a pint. You won't have time to drink a pint.' I discovered later that the closing time was somewhat erratic. This might have been explained by the number of empty Cointreau bottles in the pub dustbin.

Gill received a formal welcome to the village when there was a knock at the door. An elderly lady, Miss Lowe, presented her card and welcomed us. She had been in charge of the nurses based at Hinton House during the First World War. Miss Lowe continued to be a key member of the Parochial Church Council. She was a doughty supporter of good Victorian values. A new rector asked if central heating could be provided in the bedrooms of the Rectory, 'Central heating?' cried Miss Lowe, 'I keep my windows open winter and summer.' Needless to say central heating was not installed.

I drove every day to County Hall in Taunton while Gill, our son Richard (later known as Dik) and our basset hound Clara were left all day in the village. My commuting was a puzzle to many people. I was obviously the first person to commute in the Taunton direction, most villagers worked on the land or in local businesses, however within two years more incomers arrived and new houses were built on the kitchen garden site. Hinton House itself was bought and homes were remodelled from the west wing and the former elegant stable block.

I got involved almost immediately with the parish church as a reader, and Gill with another friend eventually ran the Sunday School. The village school itself was run by Mrs Oldfield and another full-time teacher Mrs Clifton. It was a first school, sending pupils on to the middle school in Crewkerne at the age of nine. We experienced the usual problem of keeping young people engaged with churchy things and when they reached secondary school age we started the Sunday Club which did all kinds of exciting visits and activities on a Sunday but did not require church attendance as a condition of membership.

Other newcomers were ready to join in village activities. The cricket club was revived. The once renowned drama group reappeared as Hinton Players and some of us took part in public performances of plays. An occasional club night was arranged in the village hall when various people performed with a music-hall type chairman compering the show and the retired Bishop of Plymouth tinkling the ivories. One night, when we were as usual in the pub after the show, it was suggested by the new landlord that we should revive the pantomime tradition. This we did. The village contained all the specialist skills and contacts we needed. I produced the first revival panto *Cinderella*. We obtained a smoke gun from Covent Garden. Our new publican worked there part-time behind the stage. During an afternoon dress rehearsal attended by the Evergreen Club we accidentally covered the audience with 'smoke' with a flick of the finger. Our sound and lighting people and our actors were appreciated for their skills during the production. No one knew about our day jobs. Our lighting man was head of design at the Westland Helicopter Company. The village children also played a major part in this production which added to their lifelong learning.

I had learnt to play the violin from the age of eleven and had performed weekly at the Comrades Club in my youth. At Leeds University I had played for a rapper (sword) dance team and we had participated in the Universities Folk Festival in Edinburgh. There I heard the magnificent playing of fiddlers from Dublin. This was a traumatic learning experience and after university I hung up my fiddle. Twenty years later I was given the challenge of playing the instrument again. A friend in the next village asked me to join a folk band who were playing for a local barn dance.

This was a cunning way of getting me into the band which, at the time, was short of a fiddler, the start of eight years playing regularly with them. The name of the band was the 'Five Prong Pick', a Somerset dung fork which had five prongs. Certainly we spread music around for dances in Somerset and Dorset and even, on occasion, Devon.

The family came to some of our gigs but generally I was out two evenings a week, mainly at weekends. Gill was very tolerant of my involvement with the band. Our highlights included being the support band for the tenth anniversary celebration of the 'Yetties' at Yetminster and also playing once for what seemed like hundreds of dancers in Butlins at Minehead. Eventually the demands were increased further and it may have been fortunate that we moved away from Somerset. I never joined a band again but am still actively playing at various folk evenings. In the process I have learnt to love traditional music and play it – without the written score. It will be seen that our Somerset village was a wonderful centre for family and social life.

I always worry when politicians, administrators (as was) and other innovators get attracted to the idea that education will be better if you extend the school day, ratchet up the number and difficulty of tests and examinations and create a climate of competition between schools to improve them. People learn wherever they are and no learning agency is entitled to try to monopolise the learning process. The best schools find time to promote and celebrate learning in the community around them.

In Hinton St George my professional life affected our family directly on two occasions. Gill had joined the school governing body and became chair. I was asked to go to talk to the governors about possible school closure. As a local education authority we had a policy of considering closure of a primary school when numbers fell to thirty students. Needless to say I got a dusty answer from the chair and governing body and in later years numbers increased substantially because of parental preferences from outside the village.

Another education issue affected our family life directly. One spring, our son Richard was due to spend one more year at Hinton School. There was one other pupil in his year group. Her parents wanted her to go a year early to middle school and won an appeal to the secretary of state. The head teacher advised that being a year group of one would not be in our son's best interests and he was also bright enough to go to middle school a year early. I decided that we would only agree if the appropriate test revealed him to be in the ability range agreed by the LEA for approval of early transfer. He qualified and transferred early even though on social rather than educational grounds this was not an ideal solution. Thankfully, he survived the experience. Our daughter, Katherine, and younger son, Andrew, also attended Hinton School. They all participated in the activities on offer in this hyperactive village and were taught in our small village school.

Being convinced that Hinton St George was where we wanted to stay, in 1976, Gill and I and our three children Richard (nine), Katherine (six) and Andrew (three), plus our now two basset hounds, had moved from the schoolhouse to a cottage in West Street. With two other families we had also purchased a plot of land at the end of the street so we could to keep chickens and live the good life growing our own produce. This plot eventually became known as 'Gill's Dell' and was the venue for the annual Cub Scout barbecue and bonfire.

For some years Somerset had sent secondary school students on school cruises. I was invited to be cruise leader on a joint Somerset and Wiltshire school cruise to the Mediterranean. P&O offered a free place to Gill, which was accepted with the approval and encouragement of the LEA. I would be in charge of around a thousand school children under the care of their two hundred or so teachers and Gill would also help with the various visits and activities. We decided to accept and left the dogs with relatives and the children with their favourite babysitter Myrtle Auton, and her husband Percy, at their nearby farmhouse.

P&O educational cruises were inspired by earlier trial cruises originating as long ago as 1932. The scheme developed in the early 1960s to provide cruises both in term time and in the school holidays. SS *Uganda*, on which we were to sail, took the place of earlier ships in 1967. The ship was equipped with cabins for over 300 passengers and 920 in dormitories. Some brave private passengers, heavily outnumbered by school students, also joined the cruise.

The cruise visited several classical sites but for all the students the biggest shock was to get a glimpse of a developing country. In Egypt, where we stayed one day only, I was glad that we had a rule that all students should wear school uniform. We disembarked at Alexandria and about half the buses sent to pick us up broke down on the way to Cairo. Immediately party leaders were split up from their students as individuals were squeezed into the remaining spaces on the fleet of buses. Students were able to take in the juxtaposition of jet planes and passing express trains with water wheels and simple huts in the adjoining fields. We drove back at night without headlights. We were told later that this was to hide the many Palestinian refugee camps along the route. On return to the *Uganda*, I ordered an immediate roll call and not one student was missing.

I had already seen on the United Nations Association (UNA) work camps how young people were much more engaged with social issues than the magnificent historic sites they were visiting. Getting a glimpse of the realities of life in Egypt proved to have a greater impact than the pyramids at sunset. The reaction of the students reminded me that direct experience of other cultures is an essential part of education. I had gained much from my extended national service in the RAF and as a youth officer I had seen young people grow in maturity and knowledge through the UNA work camps. Although international work camps had been around for a long time there was no attempt at national level to develop real engagement with the third world as was the case in the USA with the challenge of the Peace Corps. This remained a gap in the education of most pupils of school age.

Just before I moved from Somerset in 1985 I was appointed as one of four people who would be sent to China in 1986 to help initiate a new inspection service there. Through the encouragement of Somerset over the years I ended up with several areas of 'expertise' in no time at all. I was by now also a member of the British Education Management and Administration Society (BEMAS) eventually becoming chair and helping with their publications.

After my six-month secondment to the Audit Commission I was keen to seek a new challenge and started to apply for chief education officer posts. I applied for one in the West Country but was not shortlisted. Subsequently, I was interviewed for the post of director of education in Lincolnshire. Another recently retired chief education officer warned me that it would be a political challenge. I ignored the advice having experienced similar dire warnings when I moved from Devon to Somerset. I applied for the job and got it. It would mean a move to the east of England at a time when our eldest son Dik was taking his A levels, our daughter, Katherine, was about to take her GCEs and our younger son, Andrew, was in his last year at middle school. It was not the best time to move, so Gill stayed in Somerset for a year while I began a weekly commute to Lincolnshire.

7

from public to private –
lincolnshire to consultancy

y move from Somerset to Lincolnshire placed me in a very different political context. The differences between Somerset and Lincolnshire were considerable. Somerset had lost a third of its territory in 1974 but remained cohesive. Most members of the county council had already worked together in the 'old' county. The new Lincolnshire created in 1974 was a merger of four councils which had very different histories as local education authorities. The City of Lincoln had developed comprehensive education. The County of Holland had proudly maintained selective education. Half of the former County of Lindsey had a mixed economy which included a grammar school, which took additional students from the local secondary modern school at the age of thirteen and was said to be comprehensive. The County of Kesteven included both comprehensive and selective schools. In one town, Stamford, the grammar school places were purchased from the independent Stamford schools. In Grantham was the Girls' High School, the alma mater of the Prime Minister, Mrs Thatcher.

Since 1974 Somerset and Lincolnshire had had different experiences of the emerging practice of corporate management. In Somerset the elected members soon became dissatisfied with the 'new broom', ie the chief executive they had appointed to implement a centralised corporate management team. In contrast Lincolnshire, which had to bring together four former authorities, decided to create a strong corporate management leadership under their chief executive.

I was shortlisted for the post of director of education and went to Lincoln for interview. Applicants were accommodated in the Judges Lodging where we were attended by the steward who had once worked on the Royal Yacht *Britannia*. At dinner we met with leading members of the County Council. The next morning I enjoyed the unique experience of having tea and an ironed newspaper delivered to my room.

The interviews were thorough. During the day it became apparent that not all the elected members from the political group which controlled the County Council (Conservative) shared the same views on comprehensive education. The chair of the Education Committee seemed to be in favour of comprehensive schools but suggested that I should not say too much about them in interview. On reflection in later years this seems to have been a warning 'not to mention the war'. There were some differences of opinion on the subject within the controlling party group. A few months later the chair of education was replaced by a former chair of education from the County of Holland who was a keen advocate of grammar schools.

I was offered the post of director of education. I would start work in Lincolnshire in March 1985. This would give Gill the task of looking after a teenage family for many months by herself in Somerset.

I found accommodation in the Minster Yard in Lincoln. My 'landlord' was Canon John Nurser, the chancellor of the diocese. The Minster Yard was a lovely place to live with historic Lincoln Cathedral in its midst. It was possible to see one's home area from far away in Lincolnshire when the cathedral was illuminated.

I was seeking accommodation to rent for the family. House prices in Lincoln were much lower than in our Somerset village and we knew that one day we would want to return to Somerset where Gill's parents had moved from Devon in order to be nearer to us. A suitable solution was found. Gill's parents, Stan and Dorothy, would move into our Somerset house and we would rent a property in Lincoln. The Lincoln property offered to us was much grander than we expected but was reasonable to rent. It was the Cantelupe Chantry in the Minster Yard dating from 1350. It had enormous rooms and seven bedrooms. The family enjoyed its facilities to the full. Katherine, whose bedroom had an elegant oriel window, soon organised a sixth form party in the cellar which had comfortable sofas and a Roman wall. One day I received a call from an amused secretary to the dean and Chapter to tell me that my younger son,

Andrew, was drying his football shorts from the flagpole above our impressive battlements. Certainly the house was a good centre for entertaining but our location also offered entertainment to the many visitors who came to Lincoln. On one occasion I was photographed by a Japanese tourist as I pruned our roses.

I had been warned by a chief education officer before I applied for the post that I should avoid Lincolnshire. They said that I would be the third post holder since local government reorganisation and that there were considerable challenges. I chose to ignore the advice having been warned of trouble when I moved from Devon to Somerset. I found on taking up my post in Lincolnshire I received a warm welcome and was pleased to find an experienced and able team in the education department. I was soon to discover that I would be working in a more challenging political context than I had previously experienced.

A major review of secondary schools had been initiated. The review was led by Eddie Double, a senior education officer who had at one time held the post of acting chief education officer in the County of Holland. The review was well planned and encompassed every school catchment area in the county, both selective and comprehensive. The review was objectively looking at ways in which surplus school places could be removed.

There was a clear case for change. Lincolnshire still had a number of small secondary schools, some of them single sex. However, a strength of the county was the loyal active support of parents to their local secondary schools. All area reviews looked objectively at selective and comprehensive solutions but the firm desire of the controlling group to protect selective education made it difficult to accept change even when it would have had advantages in terms of reducing surplus places in a county which still had small, single-sex secondary modern and grammar schools. For example there was a clear case for change in the small town of Spilsby. A small grammar school and secondary modern school were neighbours and already shared facilities for school meals. The two schools worked together well. Their main problem came from the outside. Parents of students at Spilsby Grammar School chose to send sixth form students to the popular Boston Grammar Schools. One particular year Spilsby was left with a single student in the sixth form. It would only have taken a relatively small change to establish a comprehensive school for the eleven to sixteen age-range and allow sixth form provision to be made in Boston, but even this was politically unacceptable.

The main brake to change arose from the political context. Politicians in the former local education authority areas retained their fervent support for either comprehensive or selective education. No change in secondary school reorganisation had been achieved in the previous ten years and the likelihood of change was slim. There was one secondary school area where change became possible. This was to the south of the county at Stamford Grammar School where places were purchased from the independent schools in the town. A reorganisation was agreed. The secondary modern school would become an eleven to sixteen age-range comprehensive school and the college of further education in the town would provide the sixth form. Moreover, there would be savings made from no longer buying in places at the independent schools. The Audit Commission principles of economy, efficiency and effectiveness tipped the balance.

There was no general plan to close primary schools in the county given its size and rural nature but the closure of one small primary school in the fens was achieved through quite unexpected circumstances. One morning I received a request to meet the governors of a small primary school at short notice. No reason was given but I was assured that the matter was urgent and a buffet supper would be available at the school at six o'clock that very evening where a matter vital to the school would be discussed. Accordingly, I set off navigating my way across the flat lands of the south making right angled turns as necessary to avoid the waterways. I arrived in the dark at the school in its Victorian building. After refreshments the head teacher and chair of governors put a special request to me.

The previous year we had improved the facilities at a neighbouring primary school in the fens and as a result everyone wanted their children to benefit from these improvements. I was assured that the staff, governors and parents were unanimous in their desire to close their school and transfer the children to the newly refurbished school some two miles away. The head teacher who was nearing retirement age was prepared to retire. Some of the governors present were parents at the school and also wanted a change. This was probably the fastest school closure I have ever experienced. Here were no objections and the closure was quickly approved, and agreed by the Department for Education.

I had been given a major task on arrival in Lincolnshire of implementing a reorganisation which involved the closure of four divisional education offices and giving autonomy to all of the schools for their own budgets. This was a desirable objective but I felt that the small size of some schools and the lack of experience in running their budgets required a modification of the reorganisation proposals. I therefore proposed small area offices which would have an advisory and support role to help the transition to greater school autonomy. This was implemented.

Meanwhile, the Conservative government had plans for giving schools freedom from LEA control. Grant-maintained schools would receive their budgets directly from central government. At least one leading county councillor in Lincolnshire was keen to see all schools in Lincolnshire become grant maintained. He saw this as a way of reducing the burden on the ratepayers.

It was clear that there was a need to find a way of gauging the academic success of each secondary school system whether selective or comprehensive. A scheme was devised to assess the performance in each catchment area. What emerged was that the most successful schools in terms of GCE results came from selective and comprehensive areas. Similarly, there were selective and comprehensive schools at the bottom of the list. It is certain that this was a rough measure of success but it confirmed my view that there was a need to look at the quality of leadership in the schools and the quality of teaching. I do not think that the data was of any help to those who sought to retain all of the grammar schools, because significant differences in performance were revealed.

The local government reorganisation of 1974 had brought together authorities with very different political histories. This would create problems where a proposed countywide change, such as removing surplus secondary school places, was attempted. The creation of grant-maintained schools, independent of the local education authority, offered another way forward for some county councillors. This would provide release from battles over comprehensive and selective education. I had to explain that such a move would mean loss of central government grant to the LEA and would need careful consideration.

In general I enjoyed my time in Lincolnshire. Our family were well established in the rented house in the Minster Yard and the children were at the nearby Lincoln Christ's Hospital Comprehensive School. I had a good team of colleagues and enjoyed getting out to visit schools.

As director of education I was invited to represent Lincolnshire at a seminar at 10 Downing Street, ably chaired by Mrs Thatcher, for the purpose of discussing education issues with forty people from 'like-minded authorities' and also other education specialists and key Conservative politicians. The Prime Minister chaired the session well and had arranged for some ministers to sit behind her to be ready to answer questions. This was long before the development of a national curriculum, and Sir Keith Joseph was secretary of state for education. There was lively discussion. It was encouraging to attend a conference where there seemed to be a genuine desire to discuss key issues, albeit with a 'like-minded' audience.

My stay in Lincolnshire was shorter than I had expected. We were settling into life in the city and had made new friends.

I think I had not taken into account the great differences between Somerset and Lincolnshire. Size was not the problem. The difficulty of making major steps forward on surplus places and school reorganisation was compounded by the bringing together of people from four very different former LEAs. I had already been chosen to go to China for the DES in October 1986 and it was unfortunate that this coincided with the period of Education Department reorganisation. My visit with the DES team to China was badly timed.

By late 1987 it should have been no surprise to me to find myself on the receiving end of memoranda from the chief executive about my position. I had visited China with the DES team just when we were re-organising the education department. I also realised my acceptance of comprehensive education was not universally popular with the controlling political group. I recognised some of the personnel practices and tactics I had learnt about in my former roles. It was an uncomfortable start to 1988. Matters came to a head, and at this point I was glad of the support of Gill. I vacated my office one afternoon as requested. Before I got back Gill had received a call asking her to look after me because anything might happen. Immediately after the call I arrived home having completed a five minute drive and Gill was surprised to see me looking reasonably well. I hope the phone call had been intended to be helpful, if not, then it could be a good example of cynical personnel practice. A few days later Gill and I met the chief executive. I received early retirement with enhancement and began to plan my next chosen career, that of education consultant. I departed for my new career with dinner engagements and a large file of letters of goodwill.

This was a period where chief education officers were increasingly under pressure. The traditional role of chief education officer had a great deal of autonomy and elected members acted as individuals rather than in party groups. The situation changed significantly in 1974. Both officers and elected members had to learn to develop a new relationship. While we were agreed in seeking greater autonomy for head teachers, the role of the chief education officer was changing. With the development of chief executive roles, the chief education officer was expected to be part of corporate governance, advising increasingly politicised councils. This was a fundamental change in the way LEAs worked. In terms of my own career I could see that a job that had had great freedoms in the 1960s and early 1970s was changing, in that the role of the chief executive was now increasing in power, and controlling political groups were taking the lead in policy development.

The development of corporate management in Somerset in 1974 had got off to a shaky start. The politicians were unhappy with the commercially experienced and go-getting chief executive and in six months they had replaced him with a county treasurer who had already developed good relationships with the chief officers and worked collaboratively with them. In Lincolnshire, the bringing together of four administrations and politicians from four local education authorities provided a strong incentive for the controlling group to adopt a corporate approach led at officer level by a chief executive who would manage the implementation of the programme of the controlling group whatever its colour.

During my career, the role of education officer experienced a climate change with the balance of power moving from the professional officers towards the politicians. In one sense each local education authority has its own work 'climate'. In Somerset, where local government reorganisation left the remaining county intact, relationships between members and officers remained unchanged after reorganisation. Lincolnshire was an amalgamation of several authorities with different political histories. Whoever was the 'controlling' political group would have to work hard to assert control. My Lincolnshire colleagues told me that sometimes this led to some unexpected outcomes. At one point, elected members had hoped that their professional officers might be encouraged to join the then controlling political party – the Conservatives. One senior officer visited Alberta in Canada and returned wearing a red rose badge. This was mistakenly thought to be a Labour Party badge until it was explained that the rose was the emblem of a Canadian province.

During my thirty-year career in local government, the roles of education officers and elected members had changed considerably. A new profession was emerging by 1988, that of the education consultant. The offer of early retirement with enhancement from Lincolnshire County Council was a clear sign of their approval of my departure from local government. The day after my retirement from local government I was offered my first job as a consultant.

Earlier in my career any developments led to the need for additional posts in public service. Consultants were not often employed. I had gained free consultancies over the years from fellow educators otherwise the consultant was sometimes thought of as 'someone who borrows your watch to tell you the time'. In my emerging career as a consultant I soon discovered that there was some truth in this statement. A consultant could often recommend those necessary changes in an organisation that no one on the inside was prepared to suggest openly.

I was in a privileged position as were many of the new education consultants in 1988. I had been granted early retirement with an enhanced pension so I was not compelled to work in order to pay the mortgage. The number of education consultants was growing apace as financial pressures and restructuring often required redundancies and early retirements in local education departments, schools and further education colleges.

I was immediately invited to participate in a national evaluation of the Technical and Vocational Education Initiative (TVEI). I worked with another education consultant who had also recently retired as a chief education officer in another county council. I enjoyed the work which involved visits to schools and education departments. Our final report was well received and I was immediately offered further work.

This period of turbulence in the traditional role of education officers and the changes in schools produced a crop of potential education consultants. It was not long before the Society of Education Consultants was formed through the initiative of John Mann, former chief education officer in Harrow. I chaired the organisation and noticed that around ninety per cent of members left in their first year.

This was a newly emerging branch of consultancy and many people discovered the sure route to failure. This was to rent an office, lease a car, produce a widely circulated leaflet and sit in the office waiting for something to happen. Successful consultants did much more. New companies and groups were set up but there were also many successful individuals. They worked closely on their existing personal contacts in LEAs and schools. Some had already undertaken work for the DES and I was in this category. What I enjoyed about the work was the fact that the quality of one's last consultancy would determine one's success. This was a satisfying version of payment by results. All of us had an advantage not available to many consultants. We had our local authority pensions from early retirement. Later on, in 1995, when OFSTED was established and many of the senior HMIs lost their jobs, they had an even more generous retirement settlement. Some of them established or joined teams to undertake OFSTED inspections. This was to influence the shape of my own consultancy work. Doug Close, a former senior HMI invited me to join Close Associates and for several years I led secondary school inspections. I was also providing preparation for inspection advice through seminars organised by the Secondary Heads Association. My longest assignment came from the Department for Education. It provided direct experience of establishing a successful school in an area of social need. I believe it has many lessons for those attempting a top down education initiative. The next chapter tells the story of this new school in Tyneside.

8

---

the emmanuel college project

I was enjoying the roving commission given to me in the TVEI review, my first major project. It enabled me to visit a variety of schools and meet many enthusiastic teachers. Some of the results were surprising. All schools had got off to a good start in using TVEI funds to make improvements in teaching and learning. Some had lost the initial impetus because the teacher who had spearheaded the initiative had retired or moved on. The school was then left with the archaeological artefacts of innovation – equipment now unused and innovative approaches discontinued. It was obvious that the scheme had not become fully 'owned' by the school which settled back into business as usual.

As in most UK initiatives rapid results were expected and funding was short term. My incursions abroad had informed me that some other developed countries, for example in Scandinavia, had accepted that innovations needed time to get owned by educators in schools. The general expectation was that a period of two to three years was required and that people needed relevant training and support.

My consultancy work was busy but the pattern of it was about to be changed. It would concentrate my work on a single school development. I received a phone call from someone in the Department of Education and Science (DES). He asked if I would be interested in applying for the post of chief academic adviser to the sponsors of a new City Technology College (CTC) in Gateshead. I was interested even though it involved a dramatic change of role. The task would be to parachute a new school into the middle of a local education authority area. It would be seen as a threat to the viability of existing schools. Potentially I could be seen as a former gamekeeper coming into the situation as poacher of students from the local schools.

The CTC initiative had first been announced by Kenneth Baker, the secretary of state for education and science, in 1986. The scheme would establish independent secondary comprehensive schools. The idea for the initiative was inspired by a 'Magnet' school initiative in the USA. The purpose of the CTC was to establish a real choice for parents in inner city and urban areas by setting up comprehensive schools of quality outside the responsibility of the LEA. These schools for the eleven to eighteen age-range would offer a broad education with a technological and vocational bias. They would be a partnership between government and business and were intended to be a response to widespread concern about low achievement and poor schooling in inner city and urban areas.

Local businessmen in Tyneside had already come forward with a contribution to capital building costs needed to establish a CTC at Lobley Hill as an independent but publicly funded school with a clear Christian foundation.

I was invited for interview and drove to Gateshead with the intention of seeing something of the area. I made my way eastward from the Tyne Bridge towards a somewhat run-down commercial area on the Gateshead bank of the river. There I discovered the temporary base for the project in a furniture warehouse where David Vardy, the brother of the main sponsor, Peter Vardy, had his furniture retail business. David was director of the CTC project and responsible for its completion. There was no receptionist to greet me but a smiling and friendly David welcomed me into his office. My interview began immediately.

David described the development and the task of the chief academic adviser whose duties would be to help with the design brief for the building, the recruitment and appointment of staff and students, the development of the curriculum and any other matters leading to the opening of the school in September 1990. He asked me about my experience and immediately offered me the job. I accepted. The Department for Education would pay my consultancy fees and expenses and would also provide funds for me to buy in additional education specialists as required. The first task would be to design and build a CTC on the site of redundant secondary school buildings at Lobley Hill in Gateshead. We continued our discussion over a cup of coffee, and ham and pease pudding sandwiches. I was to start work as soon as possible and was allocated an office close to David's own office.

David managed the project on behalf of the financial sponsors. A project architect from Durham, Mike Lichfield, had already been appointed. I was given a consultancy budget by the DES but decided not to employ anyone on a fixed contract, instead bringing in individual consultants for specific tasks as required to advise us on detailed requirements for specialist subjects. At the end of the building project the new school was left with a residue of money to transfer into its capitation funds during the first year. I had learnt in my previous experience that some needs become apparent once the building is in use. New staff would also have their own curriculum requirements.

The sponsors had been offered the building and site of the redundant secondary school at Lobley Hill. We reviewed plans from the Architects Branch at the DES illustrating how the building could be remodelled and adapted as a CTC. The plan was completely inadequate largely because of the inflexibility of the building. I travelled to London with Peter Vardy, where we met with a senior civil servant who indicated that our plan for a new building would not be approved. Peter indicated that in these circumstances the sponsors would have to reconsider their offer of capital funds because a new build would be cheaper than remodelling. The civil servant went off to consult colleagues and returned in ten minutes with an answer. We would be able to design and build a new school but the job had to be done quickly so that the school could be opened by September 1990. The challenge was accepted.

We returned to Tyneside and made a rapid start. I worked quickly on the educational brief for the new building with the help of other specialist consultants I recruited for this task. We interviewed contractors who could prepare a design and then build the new school. We shortlisted some of them. One plan submitted looked like a bird's eye view of four helicopter rotor blades meeting at a small hub. It could be seen at once to be completely unworkable because entrances and exits were all in the hub. Around a thousand students plus staff would converge on a very small space and create an immediate people jam. The winning design from John Laing met our needs. In subsequent years it would prove to be readily adaptable. The project proceeded quickly.

It was essential now to plan for the settling of the school catchment area from which it would recruit its students. There was a need to work closely with the Gateshead LEA. The members of the council were opposed to the imposition of a new school outside their control and which offered a threat to the viability of secondary schools in Gateshead. I made early contact with the Director of Education in Gateshead, David Arbon. I had been provided with an education project officer, Eddie Stringer to assist me. He was a geographer and an experienced administrator. He lived locally and knew the area well. We arranged regular monthly meetings with David Arbon.

The CTC Trust Deed was a thorough piece of social engineering. It made specific demands on the catchment area and the make-up of the student intake. The school was to be a co-educational comprehensive school with up to 750 students in the eleven to sixteen age range. This would be extended later to 900 students. There would also be a sixth form. The aim was to recruit equal numbers of boys and girls. The ethnic balance of the area should be represented in the school intake. Two thirds of the students would have to come from economically deprived local authority wards. There would be no restrictions to admission based on race or religion. All young people in the catchment area would be eligible to apply for admission to the school. We had agreed that in order to get a truly comprehensive intake in terms of ability the National Foundation for Educational Research (NFER) eleven-plus test would be used. This would not be used to select the 'best' pupils but would provide us with a profile of the applicants in terms of ability. In practice this worked well and the social engineering that followed ensured that the intake corresponded with eight ability columns that produced a normal Bell distribution curve. This meant that many higher ability pupils who applied had to look elsewhere.

The project had a very hostile press at local and national level. This was because of its overtly Christian sponsorship. The evangelical Christian background of the sponsors was well-known. They were prominent businessmen in the north east and had sponsored other projects in the past including a hospice. The Trust Deed did not allow selection on grounds of religion or ability but many people feared the worst. The name of the CTC 'Emmanuel College', Emmanuel meaning 'God with us', also caused misgivings for some people. Before the project had been approved a high-profile event had also raised fears. A local evangelical church had processed around the redundant school site at Lobley Hill and 'claimed it for the Lord' as a site for a Christian school. This had set alarm bells ringing for some liberal clergy.

Before Emmanuel College received its first intake I was asked by the DES to check that evolution would be taught in the science faculty. It was. Only one of the eleven science staff appointed was a believer in 'intelligent design' rather than the current orthodoxy 'evolution'.

On 15th July 1988, the *Newcastle Journal* reported that the council was opposed to the establishment of a CTC in Gateshead. A spokesman was reported as saying, 'They are elitist and will definitely cream off pupils from other schools on Tyneside. They will siphon off teachers in science, technology and maths from existing local education authority schools and that will damage education for the remainder of pupils in the Borough's schools.' A spokesman for the education service in Newcastle commented, 'It is sad that the well-meaning industrialists should be encouraged to invest money in superfluous and unwanted schools… it will do nothing to resolve the challenge of providing an effective education service in the inner cities.'

The hostile reaction continued for many months. On 18th December 1988, the BBC programme *On the Record* reported as follows, 'Last week the North-East was devastated by the announcement that two shipyards are to close with the loss of thousands of jobs. It's this sort of area that the government might think would benefit from its City Technology Colleges or CTCs, new schools intended to give the next generation of inner city children a head start in science and technology. We've discovered that there is, in fact, an as yet undisclosed plan to set up a CTC in the North-East, probably here in Sunderland. It's going to be controversial. CTCs always are. But this one is going to start the biggest row yet. Its backers are evangelical Christians and they want to open a school, not just a centre of technological excellence, but equally to promote their Christian values.'

In the *Newcastle Evening Chronicle* on 23rd December 1988, John Anderson, regional officer with the teaching union, the NUT said, 'This is bringing into the system some form of selection and we think it will be to the detriment of the state secondary schools in Gateshead.'

The reaction continued into 1989 when on 8th January BBC Radio 4 recorded a Christian objection from Reverend Eddie Neil, 'It seems to me to be a waste of good Christian money.'

It was against this highly charged background that our preparations for opening proceeded very briskly. Eddie Stringer and I were keen to adhere strictly to the criteria established in the Trust Deed and recruit students for a comprehensive school, two thirds of them from economically deprived wards. We also wanted to broaden the catchment area in order to reduce the impact on existing local authority secondary schools. A decision was therefore made to recruit students from deprived wards in West Newcastle as well as Gateshead. These would provide some twelve per cent of the student body each year. Close liaison with the Newcastle LEA staff enabled us to establish a wider catchment area.

Following this decision the new principal designate made great efforts to speak to people in the catchment area. This produced a large number of applications. We had argued successfully with the DES that we would take one year group into Year 7 in 1990 and build up the student body one year at a time. It was essential to ensure the new school was up and running effectively from the start. As a result we were permitted to appoint staff well before opening the school so effective preparation and training could take place on curriculum and other matters. If key staff were appointed from several schools and also other LEAs they needed to develop as a team and also have in place a positive culture for learning, a well-planned curriculum and effective delivery of learning experiences. With this in mind it was possible to plan well for the first intake in September 1990. This subsequently proved wise in building up the ethos of the school. In all, the decision to build up numbers year by year, to recruit staff nationally and prepare well would avoid unnecessary disruption to existing secondary schools as would the decision to include part of West Newcastle in the catchment area.

By August of 1989, building plans had been completed and submitted. At the planning meeting there had apparently been considerable discussion but a small majority were in favour and, as there were no valid planning grounds for refusal, the Gateshead Planning Committee had granted planning approval, albeit reluctantly. It would be difficult for the LEA to make playing field facilities available given the opposition to the project so we made alternative arrangements to rent sports field facilities from local sports clubs.

Staff had been appointed in good time. The new principal became an effective ambassador for the school in Gateshead and Newcastle and a good team of teachers were recruited, some of them locally. We had plenty of applications. A lot of well-motivated teachers wanted to be part of the new project. Many were Christians and others who did not profess a religious affiliation were sympathetic to the aims of a new comprehensive school servicing deprived communities.

The world around us remained very nervous. The national and regional press continued to focus on potential problems such as indoctrination of students. I had already assured the DES that the science curriculum, including evolution, was fully implemented. Any other 'creation' ideas were a part of discussion in RE lessons. Once the full complement of teachers had been appointed we checked carefully to see what had been planned in schemes of work.

In terms of the expected CTC model we were departing from initial expectations. We did not implement a longer school teaching day. This was because children from difficult home circumstances needed time in school for breakfast and homework, especially where there was no effective homework space at home. We provided after-school homework rooms and access to the information technology facilities. Again, there was no need to increase time for science and technology with the teaching day itself at the expense of other subjects. The school was therefore able to offer a range of excellent extra-curricular activities. These were considered to be of high importance as were the achievements of the young people in their own leisure time as members of social clubs and groups. Years later, at the annual awards evening at the Sage Theatre, we enjoyed the arrival of a student on a motorcycle celebrating his success as a junior regional motocross champion! Any young person achieving success and enjoyment in a personal interest or activity would be more confident and better motivated at school. This strategy worked well and from the start the college newspaper would record achievements both in school and out of school. I already knew this from my own early life and my work in the youth and community services.

The recruitment and selection of students began in early December 1989 when the NFER administered their non-verbal reasoning tests. Individual scores were assigned to eight columns within the normal Bell distribution curve of ability. We had over six hundred applicants for one hundred and fifty places. It was clear that many able students would be disappointed. We decided to interview each applicant who would be accompanied by a parent or guardian. I interviewed them all in the following few weeks and was highly impressed by the motivation and keenness of students and parents. Some parents did not want their children to experience the missed opportunities and problems of their own school days. In one local authority ward the unemployment rate was fifty per cent at that time. It was clear that the school would need to provide homework and canteen facilities beyond the school day. One lad with a streaming cold dragged his mam by bus from Newcastle even though he was unwell. She said it was his idea to come to Emmanuel so she thought she ought to come along with him. Years later he would be a head boy at the school.

The interviews presented a huge range of emotions and hopes. Parental ambition, regret or desperation were part of the background to interviewing many of the potential students. Stories of lack of opportunity came through again and again. Schools, parents and students were struggling in those areas where there was a long-term experience of unemployment. In contrast families from better off wards saw this new school as an exciting new opportunity for their child. For some of the parents with academically gifted children there would be disappointment. We selected our hundred and fifty for the class of 1990 and some able young people would go to their second choice, prestigious schools in Tyneside. Our final selection gave us an excellent comprehensive intake. Two thirds came from socially and economically deprived wards. Our other criteria were also met including gender balance. The Year 7 intake for September 1990 would be a challenge.

There was a buzz of excitement on the first day of school in September 1990 as new students arrived in their uniform. The first two weeks included intensive training for students in how to move around the school. Uniform was strictly monitored each morning on arrival. Soon everyone was smartly dressed and did not have pockets bulging with all the items that should be in the school-bag. So keen was everyone, that the principal was caught out by his own vigilance later in the term. On a cold dark morning he arrived in school and sat at his desk. He always wore a suit and to his horror he discovered that he was wearing the wrong trousers. He remained firmly behind his desk until all students and teachers were in class and then shot home to change in order to comply with the rule that all teachers should be smartly dressed. During the first term everyone settled down quickly. Students walked around the building in a quiet and orderly manner. On completion of my work as consultant I was invited to join the governing body. This enabled me to see over many years the emergence of a highly successful school.

In 2000, Emmanuel College undertook a confidential survey of student attitudes. One thousand and ninety-eight students responded to the anonymous questionnaire. There were only fifty 'spoilt' papers where some students had written humorous answers. Where comments were made about staff they were aimed at those responsible for college discipline. In general several conventional perspectives of students in comprehensive schools were reflected in this survey, moving from the eagerness of Year 7 to the general negativity of Year 10 and the reflective honesty of Year 13. The findings echoed the general altruistic views of young people. Most saw the value of giving time and money to the less fortunate. Three quarters of the students had personal computers in their home and forty per cent had internet access. How far this was influenced by the school was not known.

The general public had been dubious about the impact of parachuting a potentially evangelistic institution into the area. The survey revealed that seventy per cent of those who replied to the survey believed in God and fifty-nine per cent believed Jesus to be the Son of God. Parent attitudes were not explored and they may have had some bearing on the response. Many parents seeking a faith school were attracted to Emmanuel College. The school had children from Christian, Muslim and Hindu families. Forty-seven per cent of students wished to see greater controls on the use of abortion. Two thirds of students worried about their attractiveness to the opposite sex and general popularity.

In terms of the school, seventy-seven per cent recognised assemblies as a helpful focal point for reflective thought at the start of the school day. Only forty per cent recognised that college discipline was important within a learning environment and just over a quarter thought that the college put them off becoming Christians. These and other questions asked provided only a general snapshot of student views. At this relatively early stage of the college's development as an eleven to eighteen age-range institution it enabled college management and governors to review the impact of their own work and attitudes. It would have been useful to set these views in the context of the community served by the school. This would have provided an interesting study for an education historian undertaking a community study.

It is certain that by the year 2000, the school had developed and sustained a purposeful and happy environment for learning. Inspection reports from HMI at the time provided a positive picture. Fears of a narrow and predatory faith school focused on indoctrination were thankfully not realised. It was my judgement that the sponsors had never held such a narrow view of the school's purpose but assented fully and positively to the terms of the Trust Deed.

The Emmanuel College experience as chief education adviser and governor confirmed my view that the ability and drive of the head teacher is critical. The first principal, George McHugh, brought strengths of persuasion which gave this new institution a high profile in the community and secured a well-disciplined and positive ethos. As the school grew it became important to develop a highly sophisticated curriculum and a highly skilled team to teach it. The second principal, John Burn, had proven experience as head of a large comprehensive school in Newcastle and provided the curriculum leadership which developed the school as an effective eleven to eighteen age-range institution. Emmanuel College was also fortunate to have senior staff with leadership qualities who went on to lead other schools in the emerging Emmanuel Academy Trust.

There seemed to be a need to accurately assess the stage of development of a school in order to appoint suitable leadership. Early in my career in LEAs I had experience of one or two occasions when governors were looking for a new head who was a carbon copy of the last successful one. This was not wise and on one occasion led to no appointment being made even though capable candidates had applied and would have taken the school to the next level of improvement. A continuous striving for improvement was characteristic of the Emmanuel College team. This approach had emerged as crucial to raising standards in the OECD School Improvement Project described in chapter 9. This requires from senior management the ability to motivate colleagues and build effective teams. The unanticipated impact of the arrival of Emmanuel College was an incentive for the LEA to reorganise their own schools. In future years, students from Emmanuel would have excellent educational and vocational courses on offer at their own sixth form, as well as at Newcastle College and at a newly established LEA tertiary college in Gateshead.

As a governor I was able to see another similar development in Teesside, the new Middlesbrough CTC developed in conjunction with the LEA. There was an urgent need to improve school provision. Parents who could afford to do so were sending their children across the county boundary into comprehensive schools in North Yorkshire. This development in Middlesbrough required a much more complex plan of action involving the closure of an existing comprehensive school and the immediate merger of two other schools on one site. The principal appointed for the task was Gary Wiensek who had been deputy principal at Emmanuel College from its inception. His task was enormous. Students and staff were brought together in one new school in a single move. Some teachers opted for early retirement and about one third of the teaching staff of the new school were recruited from outside. This school was also successful but gained from having a new principal with experience of new school development.

The City Technology College Trust Deed was instrumental in helping to meet the needs of areas of social and economic deprivation. Emmanuel College has remained a success and has achieved much for young disadvantaged people over the years. Its success was ensured by very clear criteria spelled out in the Trust Deed. It created a genuinely comprehensive school. This particular project enjoyed other advantages: careful use of NFER tests to achieve a balanced intake; direct meeting with individual applicants, student with parent or guardian; admission of one year group at a time to build up the college ethos; good action of staff and students and effective premises and equipment; a decision not to have an extended school day for the curriculum so that students with no homework facilities at home could use the full facilities of restaurant, library and information technology before and after the 'normal' school day. There was room to develop a lively extra-curricular programme of sports and other clubs and interest groups. Students received a general rounded education with vocational relevance. This was enhanced by social and leisure provision for students.

There was much public concern about the establishment of a Christian school with fears of indoctrination. Successive HMI reports and student surveys revealed this to be groundless. In my experience the motivation of the promoters, staff and directors was to provide excellent schooling for every student. Fairly early in its life the new school approached a local primary school and asked it to invite parents of some of their most challenging students to allow their children to come to Emmanuel College a year early. This programme worked well. It reminded me of the constant statements made by some educators early in my career that 'you cannot do much with children in this area'. That dismal assumption was proved to be wrong.

9

foreign fields – going international

I n 1980, I was settled in as a deputy chief education officer in Somerset. This promotion arose from local government reorganisation in 1974. My new job would now pitchfork me into the international study of education systems. The remaining assets of the Association of Education Committees (AEC), which had been run over by the juggernaut of corporate management and closed down in 1977, were converted into a Trust Fund to be partly used for 'other educational purposes.' The Trustees decided to establish a fellowship to be held each year by an education officer working in a local education authority. The terms of the Trust offered an opportunity to do some action research in Europe. The holder of the fellowship would be expected to spend up to three months abroad in a European country of his or her choice studying a topic of significance. A report would summarise the results of the study and its relevance to the education services. I decided to apply for the fellowship.

There was a good financial incentive. The fellow would be expected to get three months leave of absence on full salary from his employing authority and would receive an AEC grant of two thousand pounds for expenses. I also sought leave of absence from home from my wife, Gill, who would be left to look after the three children plus of course the remaining wayward basset hound.

In my application for the fellowship I proposed to visit several European countries in order to research the selection and in-service training of senior staff in primary and secondary schools. I had experience of organising and presenting training and development courses and I was confident about my choice. To my surprise I was awarded the fellowship. My journey would take me to five countries. I did not realise at the time that it would then lead on to more international work in and beyond Europe in later years.

I had modified my plans and decided to look at the selection and training of head teachers in secondary schools in five countries. I would meet people at all levels in the organisation: policy makers, training providers, local education authority officers, national representatives of teacher organisations. I would ask each country to recommend other people I should meet. These could include innovators and researchers in the field.

During my preparation I had to get a full understanding of the organisational structures of each education service. In the three Nordic countries of Denmark, Sweden and Norway comprehensive schools served both primary and secondary school students in the six to sixteen age-range. Many of them moved on to comprehensive sixteen-plus institutions. In the Netherlands there was still a selective system of education. This tripartite system included general, vocational and academic (grammar) schools. Discussions were taking place about links between the general and vocational schools. There were also a few experimental secondary comprehensive schools. In practice, several schools were bilateral or trilateral, encompassing all education offerings in one institution. In France I looked at provision in the secondary schools, in the comprehensive colleges and the lycées.

The AEC Trust asked me to explore the possibility of developing a European head teacher training course. In all the countries visited and in Britain there were several changes taking place which added considerable complexity to the role of the secondary school head teacher. These developments included a desire to delegate responsibilities to schools, ie to develop the autonomous school; greater involvement of parents and school boards, which often brought a more critical approach from the general public; a move to greater democratisation in schools evident in teachers' councils, parents' councils and class councils for students. In addition employment legislation was also bringing extra pressure to bear on head teachers. In all countries the head teacher was already affirmed to be the pedagogic leader, responsible for the quality of teaching and learning. The total of all these responsibilities indicated an urgent need for training and support for a wide managerial role. In most cases there was as yet no new job description covering all of these duties and public expectations.

Although these developments were common the variations in speed and timing of changes made it difficult to contemplate a European course at that time. There was also the issue of national history, culture and expectations which made it difficult to contemplate a common course. The greater need was to provide training and local support as head teachers implemented their school improvement plans in the workplace. General principles of how to manage and achieve improvement in schools would be a greater priority.

The detail of all the developments can be found by anyone with the stamina to read the reports I published at the time. In this chapter I have tried to provide some snapshots of my 1980 visits and my subsequent involvement in international research.

THE EDUCATION TOUR OF 1980

I started my study tour in the January. I was determined to make my expenses stretch as far as possible so I tended to travel by bus, train or boat. In the event I found all my host countries very hospitable. I made a start in The Hague. The Ministry of Education was then housed in an eighteenth-century building in the old city which was still the home of the Dutch parliament. I was welcomed warmly by colleagues in the Ministry. Two years later they would transfer to a new high rise office block between The Hague and Amsterdam which would soon be referred to as the 'Great Wall of Zoetermeer'. The old building in The Hague housed comfortable offices and an excellent library full of education books, many of them in American English. I spent several days in the Ministry and managed to read some shorter Dutch documents as well with the aid of a dictionary. My 'minder' was a young administrator, Ferry de Rijke. He gave me great help in planning my itinerary. I was able to visit schools and also spent much time with the originators and organisers of the head teacher training programme.

My visit to an experimental comprehensive secondary school in Haarlem helped me to understand the degree to which mass media and the youth culture made English a natural second language for Dutch young people. The head teacher of this school, Dr Kramwinkel and myself having concluded our discussions had lunch together in the school cafeteria. He suggested I might like to see a lesson after lunch and asked: 'what is your subject?' I said 'history'. He arranged for me to see a sixth form history lesson on the Cold War. At the start of the lesson the teacher welcomed me and the class agreed to have the whole lesson in English for my benefit. They had an impressive high-level discussion of the causes of the Cold War.

Although the Netherlands was the historic meeting place of Calvinist, Roman Catholic and Humanist traditions it became clear that it had developed a school system based on freedom of provision of education. Major legislation was rare. There had been a new education act in 1963 which was carefully implemented in 1968. It was known as the 'Mammoth Act' because of its scope and importance. Its purpose was wide ranging: to enable the Ministry of Education to exercise a stronger influence on the curriculum in its attempts to raise the general standard of education and also to meet the needs of minority groups. During my visits I found that the national curriculum and the general ethos of toleration tended to minimise the differences between Protestant, Catholic and other schools.

By 1980 the Netherlands had already established a single national training course for head teachers and deputy heads. Such training had been in the hands of various agencies prior to 1976. These courses were found to be too distant from education management for many head teachers. After many discussions and a national survey, the Ministry of Education and the head teachers' professional association established a steering group to initiate in-service education for head teachers. This was implemented by a regional training centre at Arnhem which had links to the Catholic University of Nijmegen which already provided full-time teacher training. The location may have been influenced by two of the pioneers of the project – the Minister of Education and Jan Giesbers, an education professor from Nijmegen. With the excellent Dutch road and rail networks Arnhem was a good centre for a national course. During my stay I developed great trust in the Dutch railways. One day I travelled from Amsterdam to Arnhem and had one and a half minutes to collect my post from a hotel by the railway station. I was back on the same platform to catch a direct train to Doetinghem where I was scheduled to visit the school. That evening I returned to Amsterdam in time for an early supper.

I have described the Arnhem course in my published report. The course lasted thirteen days and recruited twenty-four head teachers. One thousand seven hundred and seventy head teachers had attended the course as volunteers by 1989. There was a practice of recruiting two or three people from an individual school ensuring there was a group that could lead real change and improvement in the school. The emphasis of the course was based on organisational development theory and the focus was on the school as 'an organisation in a state of change'. The course included work to be undertaken back at school. By popular demand a follow-up course and an information centre for school organisation and management were being planned.

The teacher representatives and head teachers who attended the courses provided me with positive feedback. The course had status and recognition in schools and participants said that it had practical relevance to their work and the problems they faced in school. There still seemed to be a need for a system of support for the school once the course was complete.

From the Netherlands I moved on by train to Denmark on a cold winter's night. Denmark was a much smaller country in population and this was historically reflected in the appointment of head teachers. In former days all newly appointed head teachers had a personal visit to the monarch who wished them success. My report contains a full account of what was being done in Denmark to select and train head teachers.

A two week basic course was established for head teachers in 1973. One week was at the Communale Hojskole at Grenaa which was the local government training centre. A second week was at the Danmarks Lærer Hojskole (DLH) in Copenhagen, the national teacher training centre. Head teachers reported that they needed a 'less academic and complex course', and at the time of my visit a new course was being planned at Grenaa. The course was yet to be undertaken. Simultaneously, the DLH in Copenhagen was developing a new course which was being planned by a professor who had undertaken organisational development work with some 120 schools in Denmark.

What I saw was work in progress. Organisational development was at the basis of the new training as was the case in the Netherlands and the other Nordic countries. I was able to visit schools and see the effective work done with them using an organisational development approach. One course at Vordingborg was involving the whole staff in a school development programme. There were other examples of new initiatives. Denmark is a small country with strong personal networks. The general pattern of training provision was still developing organically.

I made a short visit to Norway in June 1980. This was my first visit to the land of my ancestors. I had by then experienced the great efficiency of trains in other countries. At Oslo station I asked a railway official what time the train to Bergen would leave. His reply was, 'we shall know the time when the train comes in.' 'Which platform?' I asked. 'We shall know when the train arrives,' he said. He went on to recommend the station restaurant and said he would let me know when it was time to board my train. Sipping a beer in the station restaurant I realised the foolishness of my question given the topography of Norway. In the winter the Bergen train would have to navigate heavy snows and some snow drifts. Even in the summer there would be goats seeking shade at the entrance to tunnels and other natural obstacles. There might even be herds of goats on the line.

This made me reflect on the difficulties of providing an education service where mountains and fjords isolate small communities. I have described the school system in my report. As in Sweden and Denmark there was a comprehensive school up to age sixteen and a post-sixteen provision. In

Norway I would discover that the attitude to the size of the comprehensive school was very different from ours. We recommended larger schools in order to deliver an economic and balanced curriculum. In Norway the concern was that no school should have more than six hundred students because it was necessary to get to know all students well.

In Bergen I met with the Education Officer Per Kvist, who was able to give me an introduction to head teacher training in Norway. The education administration had been highly centralised but was now being devolved to regions and local school boards. Head teacher training was funded nationally but was usually organised at a county and municipal level. There was a varied pattern of experimentation. Sometimes team training was provided for the whole staff in a school. Again, the organisational development approach was a basis for the training done with a view to managing change and improvement. There were both public and private initiatives. Other people I met during my stay in Norway also emphasised the need to provide a variety of solutions to meet the diverse needs in the regions.

At the time of my visit in 1980 the basic comprehensive school (Grunnskolen) head teachers had training funded nationally. Originally, residential courses of four to eight weeks had been provided but these had been abandoned because they were too costly. The current arrangements provided a basic fifteen-day course lasting a period of twelve months. Courses were residential and non-residential and people worked on projects in their own schools. They were expected to keep the staff fully informed and to draw on the experience of teachers and work with them. These school-based tasks might deal with new ways of tackling routines, giving responsibility to others and the development of team working. Head teachers and deputies attended the courses and contributed to course planning at each stage of the process.

Training was also provided for the upper schools. A course of one hundred hours was provided and between two and four people from each school were invited, including the head. Non-teaching staff were welcome to participate. Course content covered more administrative and technical training than that provided for the Grunnskolen.

I had an opportunity to look at courses in and around Bergen with schools' staff varying in numbers from three to over fifty teachers. The organisational development approach encouraged Norway and other countries to plan for long-term developments. This struck me at the time as in complete contrast to our own government initiatives which sought quick fixes. Too often these seemed to take the view of Shakespeare's Lady Macbeth's attitude to murder: 'If it were done when it's done, 'twere well it were done quickly.'

I spent six weeks in Sweden in the spring of 1980. Before I began my European visits I had read something about the national head teacher training programme in Sweden. Training had been provided for all school leaders (head teachers and deputy head teachers) from all types of school. The background to this initiative was a national commission in 1976 on the internal working of schools. This resulted in a major piece of legislation. The aim was to change teaching methods and to introduce a new school day which integrated school and community activities and gave schools greater flexibility in the use of state funds.

The idea was to 'spread democratisation'. Simultaneously another national commission was reviewing government administration of education. More would be devolved to local government.

Two new forms of training emerged as a result of the 1976 reforms. Both were aimed at the leadership in the school. Training was provided for school teams over ten days in a year involving courses aimed at the understanding of the local society context and involving some work in school. The separate school leader programme was compulsory for head teachers and deputies and provided a two-year programme which included twenty-five residential days as well as home-based sessions. The emphasis of the course was on developing working practices with staff in the school. My report describes the scheme as I observed it. It was a fully-fledged national programme of training to create the desired changes and improvements in schools. As elsewhere in the Nordic countries the basic approach was based on organisational development.

I arrived in Stockholm by air in April 1980. The good weather enabled me to get some idea of the beauty of the city and its surrounding archipelago. I travelled south by train to Linköping where the school leader education programme had its headquarters. I was met at the station by Eskil Stego, the director of school leader education who took me to the best five star hotel in town. Subsequently I informed my Swedish colleagues that I was on a fixed expenses allowance and was attempting a highly ambitious travel programme so I had already transferred to a more modest but comfortable guest house not far from the hotel.

I need not have worried. Swedish hospitality was fulsome and included supper parties where we would all go home by taxi because of the strict drink driving laws and penalties. I soon met Nils Lagervall, a school leader member of the organising team, and on the first Sunday in Linköping I attended the Lutheran Church with him. The team had worked out an excellent programme of visits to courses, schools and individual education specialists.

I learnt that the school leader training programme had been carefully planned but needed some modification from the start. A move had been made rapidly from an administrative training programme to training based on school organisational development. This involved non-directive sessions based on the kind of social group work training that I had encountered in the youth service in England. This non-directive approach did not go down well with some long-serving and experienced school leaders. The compulsory nature of the training did not help matters and it was decided that school leaders within a year of retirement need not attend the course. The programme had received full support across the political spectrum. The aims of the legislation seemed ambitious but provided school leaders with the knowledge needed to improve schools.

The course planning was supported by some university researchers. Mats Eckholm, from the University of Gothenburg, provided much of the training in social science theory for the trainers on the course. I had a high regard for his work and in 1981, when I had completed my report, I invited Mats to England to evaluate some regional head teacher training we were developing in the south west.

He made a devastating but helpful evaluation of what we were attempting to do. The course content was not meeting the needs of most participants. The best value would be to enable head teachers to meet each other regularly to discuss key issues and compare their experiences of implementing change. This encouraged us to support regular meetings of secondary school head teachers. These meetings provided an effective stimulus to head teacher development.

The training teams in Sweden benefitted greatly from the support given by the directing team in Linköping. Evaluation of teacher training was a key concern for educators in Sweden. They did not have an external examination system in secondary schools so school evaluation was not narrowed down to examination league tables. Careful analysis and evaluation of schools was characteristic of the Swedish approach. There was a clear strategy for evaluation of outcomes at all levels in the education system. This included the assessments by the Swedish National Audit Board who looked at goal achievement costs and effectiveness. The evaluation of this particular leadership programme was that limited success had been achieved in terms of school development but that there had been a significant impact upon the professional development of the school leaders. Comparison had been made with similar evaluations in the USA and Canada. It was refreshing to see such willingness to learn from studies in other countries. Indeed the Swedish school leader training programme was the most ambitious one I observed in 1980. There was a serious attempt to evaluate the effects of the programme. Trainers were prepared to assess their own work and take criticism from others in search of greater effectiveness. The Swedish attempt to improve schools was nationwide and well resourced, but it was also realistic in that it recognised the length of time needed to implement and establish a major change in a school. This seemed to contrast with the over optimism or naivety of some British politicians who were personally anxious to find quick fixes.

My final visit which was to France was relatively short. It was clear that there were some good training courses and there was a move to give greater authority to head teachers. The visit is also recorded in my AEC reports and owed much to the help of Regional Inspector Michel Soubry. This visit confirmed that France was addressing the same problems as other countries. The response had been a regional pattern of courses for head teachers. France had also developed an excellent bank of case studies for use in head teacher training. I observed a course in Nantes where head teachers were glad to get support for their new expanding responsibilities.

I soon published my report to the AEC Trustees. It was widely published and led almost immediately to my being seen as an 'expert', a most unexpected outcome of my grand tour.

10

---

learning from international studies – the creation of the instant expert

Comparative education studies are subject to many pitfalls. Those based upon visits undertaken in a relatively short period of time can only provide a partial picture as seen through the researcher's own background knowledge, experience and personal priorities. Each of the education systems observed had been shaped by its own national context. A researcher coming up with new ideas based on a short study can quickly become acknowledged as an 'expert' in the field. This happened to me soon after my AEC report was published.

I received an invitation to address a Council of Europe seminar on head teachers at Windsor and soon afterwards a head teacher training conference in Milan. Over the years I was invited to other research conferences. I compounded the felony by organising a joint European Conference in 1982 in conjunction with the National Association of Head

Teachers (NAHT) and the Association of Teachers in Europe. This attracted representatives from nine European countries. I wrote articles for journals and the University of Oslo translated my report. It was particularly pleasing that our family's ancestral home country took the trouble to put my work in the university library.

I tried to keep up to speed with the changes taking place in the countries I had visited. The greatest differences between the national training schemes were due to the degree of autonomy given to the schools. In a system that provided detailed regulations the training had to cover administrative matters. There were many good examples of training based on organisational development, which attempted to bring about and sustain real change and improvement in the school.

In all of the countries I had visited, the training and development of head teachers and deputies was considered worthy of substantial investment. A course had to take place over a reasonable length of time if real improvements were to be secured for students, parents and teachers. The Swedish assumption that it would take two and a half years to effect real change in a school seems to me to be the most realistic assumption: so different from our British desire to attempt rapid and economical reforms to schools.

The recruitment of head teachers remained a universal problem in Europe. Sometimes incentives and remuneration were inadequate and people had to be persuaded to move out of their comfort zone into headship. There had been some successful recruitment campaigns. In Stockholm women were persuaded to apply for headships. When I first visited in 1980, most head teachers in Sweden were male. A specific initiative to recruit women in Stockholm County had resulted in fifty per cent of headships going to women. This was a project devised and driven by an impressive woman inspector of schools in the county, Ingemar Horth Ackerman.

There was no real shortage of men and women capable of becoming head teachers. Many people grew in the job after appointment and the increasing availability of preliminary training for headship would encourage more to apply for headship posts. The Project on School Improvement (POST) in England and Wales had identified best practice in head teacher selection.

My AEC fellowship opened up a continuing involvement in international education even though my report conclusion did not suggest a European training course, as at least one trustee had hoped. In 1981, a major OECD initiative was launched by the Netherlands. The Project on School Improvement was deliberately shaped to involve teachers, trainers, head teachers and education administrators in collaborative studies. UK involvement was proposed and I was asked to prepare a UK submission to the OECD. I had already been involved in the work of a small group from the Society of Education Officers and the European Forum (SOE/EF) to prepare a proposal for a series of international exchange seminars on the subject of head teacher and senior staff training in schools. As a result of my submission the SEO/EF proposal was merged with the Dutch one as a strand entitled: 'School leaders as change agents in the school improvement process.' This proved to be a popular OECD initiative which linked various institutions in co-development activities in fourteen countries worldwide. I became chair of this group and was succeeded, when I took up my post in Lincolnshire, by Shirley Hord from the University of Texas, USA. As part of the OECD programme, delegates from various countries visited head teacher training programmes in the UK. One of these was in the south west which I had helped to initiate and organise.

By 1984, the co-development programme had stimulated very many bilateral links. One key participant was the National Development Centre for School Management at the University of Bristol, headed up by Dr Ray Bolam. It was a surprise that our training initiatives in England and Wales seemed better known worldwide than in our own country. This may say something about the way in which we failed at the time to spread news of successful training initiatives in our own country. In the early 1980s, the Department of Education did not have the advantages of a single major piece of legislation such as those in the Netherlands and Sweden but was constantly focusing on the varied but short term initiatives of national politicians.

This opportunity to see education provision elsewhere helped me to confirm my own views on head teacher training. I was convinced that the in-service training of a head teacher should focus on the trainee's own school's specific plans for effective achievement of school improvement. Training should build confidence and must also involve the briefing and training of the whole school staff. Where some other national initiatives were based on an understanding of the principles of organisational development to achieve improvements, we in England and Wales managed to make our way to understanding the needs incrementally. It is interesting that the one element of school improvement of no interest to the DES was the preparation of a 'conceptual map' for the project, to help determine the links between the various elements and the desired results. The British response was 'we do not do conceptual maps.' In a sense this was an eloquent example of the British preference for making separate and continuous efforts to find something to improve schools rather than creating a longer-term strategy.

One achievement of the OECD International School Improvement Project (ISIP) was the long-term involvement of teachers and head teachers in international programmes. One of the reports published in 1987 on the 'Role of the School Leader in School Improvement' was from the group I originally chaired. The majority of the work was done by my successor, American Professor of Education Shirley Hord, and the dynamic people who brought experience and wisdom from several countries worldwide.

11

inspection and other performance measures

No inspector called when I was at Bridgnorth Grammar School. During the Second World War inspectors were on active service. In the late 1940s and early 1950s visits from Her Majesty's Inspectors were rare. There was a rumour that an inspector had called at the grammar school once while the headmaster was picking strawberries in the school garden but perhaps this was just an apocryphal story based on our admiration for the headmaster's affable and laid-back approach to life. We knew that he did not like external interference. At one point in the late 1940s, he gathered up numerous county letters and circulars and posted them all back to county hall. There were no repercussions.

During my time in Devon and Somerset I had considerable contact with our own local advisory teams but never encountered an HMI. I knew that Her Majesty's

Inspectors were often fully involved in national initiatives and curriculum studies at a time of expansion and change in the education service. Their national reports were held in high regard, being seen as independent of political influence and generally well researched. Local advice and monitoring of standards was the task of local education authority advisory and inspection teams. In 1984, my work with the Audit Commission required discussions with HMIs. Our Audit Commission team also presented our findings to a major HMI conference in the same year. This event was an opportunity to discuss our findings with HMIs who used them as part of their support and advice to schools.

Throughout my career in education my preoccupations were to do with expansion and growth, both institutional and individual. Within the rapidly expanding youth service there was a desire to extend young people's horizons and prepare them to make better use of the increasing leisure time that would be available to them. It was believed that more leisure would provide a richer life for the individual; what one leading youth specialist described as 'a life full of meaning'. In my study of head teacher training the emphasis was on improvement of the capacity of leaders at a time of education expansion and change. Work on a rapidly expanding school building programme also focused upon the need for better buildings and facilities. Schools were seen as natural promoters of community activities. Comprehensive schools would provide lifelong opportunities for learning in the community. Schools would be agents of education opportunity and social mobility. At this time of reorganisation and expansion, less attention had been given to the quality of education provided in schools. Our task was to build and provide opportunities.

As yet debate about the curriculum was still to develop. The Great Debate of the late 1970s attracted very small numbers at evening meetings across the county of Somerset. The debate may have interested the few but had not yet fuelled the later political preoccupations with the content of education. The new national curriculum and a call to raise standards would bring a need for more monitoring, more assessment and more school inspection: proof for parents and politicians that standards of education were rising behind all the activity.

In Somerset, I was preoccupied with management of education budgets and a review of school places at a time of retrenchment. It therefore needed something unusual to turn my attention to inspection as a matter of concern. The catalyst turned out to be a major request to Britain from a foreign power.

In 1984, I had accepted the post of director of education for Lincolnshire. It was at that point, in my final months with Somerset, that I received an unexpected call from a senior civil servant at the Department for Education and Science. I was invited to join a team of inspectors who were to assist China with the reintroduction of a system of school inspection. The Chinese authorities had sounded out both the Russians and the Americans who apparently claimed that they had all the answers and would be pleased to pass on their extensive experience. The British said they did not know whether they could deal with all the issues but that they would be pleased to help if asked. The Chinese authorities accepted our modest offer, no doubt thinking the British must be 'our kind of people'. They may already have had some distant memories of HMI visiting British schools in China prior to the Japanese invasion in the 1930s.

Having moved to Lincolnshire in March 1985, in the autumn of 1986 I joined the British team for their initial three week visit to China. The team was led by Pauline Perry, at that time Her Majesty's deputy chief inspector of schools, other team members being Alan Turberfield, an HMI staff inspector and Alan Barraclough, chief inspector of the Inner London Education Authority which would soon be reorganised out of existence. Together we made a diverse 'gang of four'.

In Beijing we were met by Chinese officials who took us to a hotel in the city where we had our preliminary meetings. We were then taken to see a large high school in Beijing where we visited classes and saw the Chinese tradition of school eye exercises which took place each day in class. I sat in on a sixth form history lesson. The students were enthusiastic and keen to engage in discussion. They displayed good command of the English language. Some of the students told me that they visited the city parks in order to seek out English speaking tourists and converse with them. This helped them to improve their English accent and vocabulary. There was a large map of the world on the classroom wall and the teacher asked the students to find England. This particular map projection had China right in the middle and in the top left hand corner was a very small British Isles.

The Chinese, like ourselves, would always take foreign visitors to their best schools. I soon discovered another similarity. Some of the high school students demonstrated familiar adolescent traits. During the mid-morning break at this high school all the students were expected to go down to the playground for physical exercises. A group of boys could be seen watching the proceedings from windows on the fourth floor. An announcement was made and I asked my interpreter to translate the message. It was this: 'Come on Year Ten, we have foreign visitors with us today and you ought to make an effort to join in.' The school applied gentle persuasion rather than the threat of punishment.

After our introductory visit to Beijing we took a plane to Wuhan which was to be the venue for our official discussions. We were to be based in a traditional hotel on the banks of the Yangtze River at the very spot where, in 1966, Chairman Mao took a dip to show how fit he was. This was the very hotel where he himself had stayed. We were the first European visitors to Wuhan since before the Japanese invasion. The Western attire of our leader was of great interest to elderly women in the street near our hotel who stopped to feel the texture of her clothing.

We were each allocated a personal interpreter for our discussions. The chief interpreter was a former professor from the University of Wuhan who had been demoted to become caretaker of a block of flats during the Cultural Revolution but was now principal of the prestigious English language high school in Wuhan. The interpreters did a good job but the youngest and least experienced one had to be corrected by the chief interpreter from time to time. On one occasion the chief interpreter had to intervene to say, 'our visitor did not say yes, he said no.' This young interpreter was assigned to HMI Alan Turberfield, our staff inspector. As we said goodbye the interpreter solemnly said, 'I would like to thank you Mr Tuberfield for your intolerance.' Thankfully, after our weeks of discussion, Alan understood what he really intended to say.

We had met with education officials from seventeen of China's twenty-five provinces. They were a diverse group which reflected the diversity of the country. Western-suited academics from Shanghai and a traditionally garbed blue suited man from Inner Mongolia with his tea caddy reflected the range and diversity of the delegation and the country itself. This enormous education service was dealing with both first and third world conditions. We were based in Hubei Province and I asked an official how many teachers there were in the province. He replied, 'two hundred and forty-eight thousand'.

'That many teachers?' I exclaimed.

'No', he replied, 'that is the number of schools.' He went on to explain that in addition to the many school buildings there was also an enormous army of peripatetic teachers who carried school in their backpack. These individual educators surmounted great obstacles and walked long distances to small numbers of pupils in mountainous areas.

In Wuhan we visited a primary school which incorporated a nursery school. The twelve hundred students welcomed us into the school waving British flags with a loud cheer. The principal said that the main problems were experienced in the nursery classes. China's one child policy meant that when they arrived at school the children had previously been cared for by doting grandparents while their parents were out at work. The teachers then had the challenging task of encouraging these 'little emperors' (and presumably 'little empresses') not to fight each other for toys but to cooperate. In contrast some older students entertained us with impressive performances of classical Western and Chinese music on various musical instruments and demonstrations of sporting skills, Chinese art and table tennis. This all-round virtuoso performance led to a discussion of selective schooling; the Wuhan schools were selective at all stages. There was competition to get into nursery, primary, junior high and senior high schools. Students were then directed to appropriate courses at university.

China is a huge country full of many ethnic groups with some two hundred languages. The diversity of the people of China was evident when we joined great crowds on the Great Wall of China. In Hubei Province alone where we were based, there were forty-eight million inhabitants living in great cities at one end of the spectrum and remote mountain dwellings at the other. I visited the Iron and Steel Works in Wuhan. They had recently upgraded their technology and downsized their workforce from 300,000 to 200,000. I saw a woman computer operator controlling and monitoring the whole operation on her computer. This huge enterprise financially supported twenty schools in the Wuhan area.

I was informed that permission was required to travel beyond one's own province. This seemed like tight political control of the population however the size of the population meant some control was needed to prevent millions of province dwellers all descending in one go on Beijing. The real limitation at that time seemed to be transport. The bicycle was personal transport for most people and there was no sign of heavy motorised traffic in the cities.

In one Wuhan school I sensed some political change in the air. Every Friday in every school the political officer would read from the obligatory party newspaper. I was there in the staffroom on a Friday afternoon, the bulletin was read but I was told that the reading was preceded by an encouragement to get on with something else while the ritual was performed.

It was clear from our visit that China would build an effective school inspection service. They were amazed that our own education legislation at that time gave detailed attention to transport entitlement, collective worship and school dinners but omitted to lay down a national curriculum. That would soon change.

My early retirement from Lincolnshire and new career as an education consultant occurred as a huge number of reforms were made in the education service in England and Wales. At the time I gave talks about the Great Education Reform Bill (GERBIL) characterising the reaction of local authority officers as HAMSTER (Horrified Administrators Mesmerised by Sudden and Traumatic Education Reform). Schools were given greater autonomy and were also being encouraged to opt out of local authority control. The promotion of 'parental choice' and increased responsibility for school governors added to the turbulence in the system. A national curriculum was established, and the need for monitoring its roll-out and its detailed requirements led to a remodelled and expanded inspection service through privatisation. This would also affect local education authority inspection services.

Nine years after introducing our inspection system to China HMI had a major reorganisation and OFSTED (the Office for Standards in Education) was born. This major change provided redundancy or early retirement to half of the HMI team and created a new system where inspection was privatised. Inspection providers would bid for contracts and Registered Inspectors would lead inspection teams.

I had not considered a career in inspection. In 1992, I had completed my major consultancy in Tyneside and had returned to Hinton St George. I was invited to stand as county councillor and had the experience of returning to County Hall in Somerset, this time as a member of the Education Committee. This meant that I could now claim to be both poacher and gamekeeper, though the balance between those two roles had changed dramatically over the years. Basically, officers and members had the freedom to choose to be both poacher and gamekeeper in the new 'Game of Thrones' where officers were losing some freedoms and elected members were seeking more control of education policy and development.

I was settling into my new political duties when I received a phone call from a former HMI, Doug Close, who invited me to join his secondary school inspection team at Close Associates, which I did gladly. Initially I inspected history and management aspects but was soon asked to become a Registered Inspector and lead inspections. As a result of this I also gained new consultancy work helping schools to prepare for inspection by means of seminars promoted by the Secondary Heads Association.

When the new inspection guidelines were published I was apprehensive about their impact. They were very detailed and comprehensive in their coverage. At the last minute Eric Forth, the minister of state for schools had added a section on the spiritual, moral, social and cultural education of young people. Some inspectors were sceptical and there was at least one spoof report: 'There was evidence of awe and wonder, especially on the walls', which described the graffiti in a school. In reality however, this late addition to the guidelines brought them right into line with the broad aims of the 1944 Education Act. Although politicians and the public were anxious about examination results and standards I was glad to see these 'soft' non-statistical aspects given prominence. I was aware that these were the very conditions that underpinned school experience and helped to deliver a rounded education and good examination results. I had seen very successful selective and comprehensive schools which based their teaching and learning on sound principles of all-round development. The minority of schools, schools that made themselves 'crammer' schools would leave their students 'cabin'd, cribb'd, confin'd' (Shakespeare quote). At this time secondary school inspection lasted a week but schools were given six weeks' notice and were able to meet the registered inspector to provide information in advance.

The inspection teams I led were highly professional and included a number of former senior and experienced HMIs one of whom inspected school management and English. She was marvellous at encouraging teachers. Although the guidelines said that we should inspect and measure and not advise we did set this requirement in a positive context.

Teachers, like students, need a positive and encouraging atmosphere in order to improve. This same former HMI was also helpful in liaising with monitoring inspectors who came to see us at work. On one occasion she joked: 'If he gives us any trouble I'll sort him out, after all I trained him in his job.'

I led an eventful inspection at a secondary comprehensive school in London where the head teacher was about to depart to become head of a new purpose built comprehensive school elsewhere. On the first day of the inspection I was informed that we were to have a visit from a monitoring HMI who was to be accompanied by the secretary of state for schools. The monitoring inspector asked the head teacher and me to put together a programme for the minister. He was coming to see an OFSTED inspection following a debate in the House of Commons. This was a tall order at short notice nevertheless the head teacher came up with a brilliant idea. We knew that the minister was interested in history so we arranged for him to sit in on a Year 8 class who were doing a historical study of a key event where they were to find out who was responsible for what had occurred. This was an exciting 'who done it' project that involved a lot of investigative work by the students. The day of inspection arrived. After watching the first lesson the minister had coffee and asked if he could go back and watch the concluding lesson where the results would be revealed. This was arranged with the permission of the teacher who in my opinion deserved a medal. That evening, a Thursday, was the occasion when the inspection team drew up their main findings and key issues for improvement. Once the major decisions were made we opened our usual bottle of red wine. The minister joined in enthusiastically. Sadly the monitoring inspector had to limit his intake because he was driving. Some weeks later Hansard reported that the minister had been pleased by his recent visit to a secondary school inspection and that the OFSTED system seemed to be going very well.

Alongside my inspection work I was leading day seminars on preparing for inspection. I had undertaken an evaluation of head teacher training and selection for the SHA (Secondary Heads Association) in the early 1990s and now presented these seminars for them. Preparation was essential for head teachers and when it was well done it helped the inspection team to progress quickly with their work in the school.

In this new OFSTED framework the inspection team had preliminary information from the schools some weeks in advance. The registered inspector visited the school for a preliminary discussion with the head teacher and the team worked out the particular areas of concern that should be explored. Although some head teachers and staff were concerned about this time-consuming preliminary work others welcomed an early opportunity to meet the registered inspector. It was a chance to demonstrate the strengths of the school and to inform the school's own actions in preparation for the inspection. A newly appointed head teacher might welcome this early meeting. In one case, I met with a recently appointed head teacher who had succeeded a popular 'strong' teacher with a national reputation. The previous inspection had produced a good report however she had been proactive in her new role and had discovered some problems which had arisen. She expressed the view that her predecessor had improved the school markedly but he had not delegated some key tasks. In the period following his departure and before a new head teacher was appointed some aspects of leadership and management had deteriorated. She had also examined the previous inspection report and had concluded that the inspecting team had been unduly influenced by the existing reputation of the school and the head teacher and had not addressed some potential problem areas. Her candour helped to identify areas of further improvement and provide the new head teacher with a platform from which she could build up a school leadership team. In this particular case her initial diagnosis proved to be accurate.

In another school the newly appointed head teacher had not briefed us about any problems but it was clear during the inspection that a long-serving senior member of staff was acting as a roadblock to necessary change and improvement. The need to improve school leadership and management was evident during the inspection week, which was the very first week in which a school could now be identified as having serious weaknesses without having to be put into special measures. It was clear that this school had a major problem but under the new leadership had the capacity to tackle it. The inspection report gave the head teacher a powerful aid to move things forward.

In general, if a school had serious undeclared problems or tried to hide shortcomings the wheel usually fell off by the second day of the inspection because these matters would soon be picked up by an inspection team. Our inspection team management aimed to be firm but fair and encouraged teachers to use inspection as a positive tool for school improvement. As individuals we were sometimes invited back to share in a major school celebration. In my case I attended the opening of a new sports hall at a school where the senior students had been proactive by writing directly to politicians at local and national level and in encouraging the local community to press for the project. The opening day was enhanced by a procession led by the school Sikh band. The sports hall was there partly because the school had encouraged well-informed and proactive citizenship.

Throughout this period I continued to follow international developments in the field of school improvement. I was invited to write a book about management competencies. The world of education had often seen books about leadership competencies but we had little knowledge of the historical background. The USA had led the field in researching the reasons for the success of superior performers in business during the 1920s. Studies of the competencies of superior performers had looked at the qualities, skills and behaviours of effective managers. Leadership effectiveness was traditionally defined by such criteria as 'subordinate commitment to task objectives' (taking people with you?), and 'subordinate satisfaction with the leader.' A vital test was: 'the success of the leader's group or organisation in performing its mission and attaining its objectives.' This early American research identified the 'traits' of successful leaders. These included self-confidence, the need for socialised power, the need for achievement, the desire to compete with peers, respect for authority figures, tolerance for high stress, a high energy level, interest in oral persuasive activities and relevant technical conceptual and interpersonal skills. All those were a requirement for the American business context but in our own context and culture such a list of leadership qualities would be traumatic for many.

From the 1920s onwards, there were many studies of the necessary competencies and it was possible to build up a long list of requirements which many of the great and the good in past history would have found challenging. Indeed most people would not have the stamina to work with the superhero described by the list of competencies. There was also some aversion to competency models in the USA. In the 1960s an attempt had been made to develop competencies for trainee teachers but this proposal had met with fierce resistance.

By the 1970s, the National Association of Secondary School Principals (NASSP) in the USA had produced a more manageable list of competencies. As in other attempts there was neglect of a key element, ie the values and assumptions underlying the model. The American business management approach model did not fit in with the needs of a school offering a broad and balanced education. I found competency models helpful in some of the work I did with the SHA assessment centre at Oxford Brookes University. My conclusion was that the best place to develop management competencies was within the school, as I showed in my book written in 1993. In the early 1990s generic management standards were being developed in

Britain. These standard competencies addressed the basic knowledge and skills required for 'average performance'. This was not a means of building a picture of a British superhero.

The danger with all-singing, all-dancing management initiatives is a search for universal all-embracing models. Earlier initiatives such as 'Management by Objectives' failed to last in the end because they were so time-consuming. In some enterprises the annual review became a necessary chore and not the real driver of improvement and change. Participants in over-elaborate and time-consuming management tools soon back off. They end up suffering from a well-known disability MEGO (Mine Eyes Glaze Over). Competencies can be useful if set in the context of a school's ethos and purpose and applied judiciously and sparingly, not least in job and personnel specifications and the personal and professional development of individuals. My experience of inspection helped me to understand that real improvement can only come from within the school. External agencies can legislate, encourage and assess but the real drive needs to come from within the organisation.

12

---

untrodden career paths –
music and politics

I rejected a full-time career in either music or politics. For many years I played the fiddle in a Somerset Ceilidh band playing what a friend of mine called 'cross-country music'. Gill and the children supported me in this all-embracing hobby. The band was called The Five Prong Pick, the name of a Somerset dung fork which was quite appropriate. We were actively spreading music about in Somerset and occasionally parts of Dorset and Devon working with several different callers. We were the support band for the 10th Anniversary in Yetminster of the more famous band The Yetties. Our kind of dance music would never hit the high spots however and we did not seek to go professional. Our music would never reach the Top Twenty.

I once turned down the chance of a career in politics. A long-serving Liberal candidate had fought the Yeovil constituency for years. I had no participation in local political activity but always lent a hand at general elections for parliament. When our candidate retired I was asked to consider standing but decided against. I did not see myself enjoying life in politics as much as my work in education. I was glad when Paddy Ashdown was selected to fight the seat and won it. Gill and I were very active in his campaign and continued to support him thereafter. My move to Lincolnshire in 1985 stopped our active involvement.

We returned to Hinton St George in 1992. I was still engaged in education consultancy and had no thoughts of standing for a political appointment either paid or voluntary, however once news of our return was noticed by the Liberal Democrat constituency office I had a visit from a friend who was working as their agent. In the following year, 1993, the Liberal county councillor who had a majority of forty-seven was retiring. The friend, Les Farris, asked me if I would stand as their county council candidate for our Dowlish Wake Division which had around five thousand electors and was tucked away in the countryside between the three towns of Chard, Crewkerne and Ilminster. This was a kind of Bermuda Triangle where tourists would sometimes get lost when the signposts ran out. I agreed to take on the challenge and accordingly I began canvassing for the county council election of May 1993.

The main county council elections tended to have low turnouts of around thirty per cent. However, in our division of five thousand electors, many communities achieved fifty per cent. Holding the seat would require a lot of visiting and canvassing. The Conservatives controlled the council and would be my main opponents. I made an early call at a cottage in the woods where I almost stumbled over the well in my search for the front door. I was received with great joy. I was the first politician ever to call for any election, district, county or constituency. I was offered a cup of tea and promised a vote, which was almost a vote of thanks for calling.

Very occasionally all did not go smoothly. I had my ankle nipped by a West Highland terrier at a house where the owner was out. There was also an occasional threat from the electors themselves. I knocked on the front door of a former council property in one of the larger villages. A very tall and extremely wide man bellowed a direct question, 'What do you want?' I explained that I was the Liberal Democrat county council candidate. 'You Paddy's man then?'

'Yes' I admitted.

He continued, 'If you had been the bloody Tory and were on fire on my doorstep I wouldn't piss on yer to put 'un out.' I assumed I had his vote and moved quickly on to the next house. In that 1993 election I increased my majority to 180 and also found myself a member of the majority group on the county council. So I began my new part-time role as a county councillor. No doubt some of my former professional colleagues would be wondering whether I had arrived to help them or haunt them.

In 1993, the familiar county council committee structures were still in place. I became chair of the Schools Sub-Committee. This was a new experience for me, being part of the political structure which I had advised for decades. The Liberal Democrat controlling group had certain core policies but the party line was exercised to provide some freedom for individual councillors. We were allowed a free vote on matters specifically concerned with the division we represented. This was helpful especially if the council was proposing a school closure in the Division. It was the job of the county councillor to represent the views of the community affected by the proposal.

Trouble could arise where an individual councillor proposed a major change to full council without consulting the party group. I experienced the result of such action at a quarterly meeting of the full county council. A prominent member of the controlling Liberal Democrat group put a motion to full council moving the abolition of stag hunting on the Quantock Hills. This was a matter which many members of the public supported as did individual councillors across the party groups. On the way in to the meeting I had seen the former Conservative chair of the Schools Sub-committee holding a banner proclaiming 'Stop Stag Hunting'. Abolition of hunting was supported by many of our party group but the ambush proved difficult for some of our members who had relatives working for the hunt. It would seem like a call for the turkeys to vote for Christmas. In the end a small majority of the full county council voted not to implement the change. The proposer's objective was not achieved but the whole debate brought local politics to life even though we shot the proposer's fox and continued to shoot the deer as well.

The county councillor is kept busy dealing with problems raised by individuals. In the Yeovil constituency the regular surgeries organised by the MP would be attended by the local district and county councillors. Other matters would be raised at parish council meetings which I tried to attend regularly.

There were twelve parish councils in my division which varied somewhat in the management of their business. In the largest parish the chair was a retired senior naval officer. He ran a tight ship and the parish council covered the agenda well. He made sure that every member of the parish council had their say and was not afraid to stop anyone taking more than their fair share of discussion time. It was customary for the local district and county councillors to present their reports at parish council meetings. I received a phone call from the chair to ask if I would mind preparing a short written report for each meeting. This would enable him to ask the district councillor to do the same. He was a good councillor but had a tendency to go on at length about his enthusiasms and stray beyond the agenda for the meeting.

As a county councillor I was able to compare the performance of members of parliament when they were asked to deal with the problems of individual constituents. Three of the five county MPs were like terriers, snapping at the heels of the county council when fighting the case of an individual. We never heard a thing from the other two. Perhaps they were not comfortable with casework and delegated to others. Two of the most active MPs were Paddy Ashdown, leader of the Liberal Democrats, and Tom King, a Conservative Minister of Defence. The best champions were those with the greatest responsibilities.

I stood for county council again in 1997 and increased my majority to 584. The Liberal Democrats had four fewer councillors but still held a clear majority and control of the council. I was made chair of a new Education Review Committee. It was our task to scrutinise policy proposals coming before the Education Committee, the committee members representing all three parties Conservative, Labour and Liberal Democrat. The committee was a means of taking an objective view of matters such as school reorganisations and closures and the effect that proposals would have at grass-roots level. At this time of financial constraint we also examined the likely impact of budget cuts. In 2001 I was invited to stand again, but I had always considered that councillors should retire at the age of seventy at the latest. There were some boundary changes for county divisions and I would be seventy in the next quadrennium. All the parties had difficulty in recruiting younger councillors. At that time all our meetings were during the daytime. In the eight years I served as a county councillor, two young councillors, one Conservative and one Liberal Democrat were pressed to resign by their employer and we lost two active and promising local councillors.

When I stepped down as county councillor in 2001, I was asked to chair the South Somerset Strategic Partnership Committee as independent chair. This committee brought together county and district council representatives and representatives of public services such as police and fire, representatives from local industry and commerce and the voluntary organisations. This was a temporary role for me while this new body was building up its own arrangements for promoting and stimulating developments in South Somerset.

Meanwhile changes were taking place in the county council. This was part of a move at county level to develop a form of 'cabinet government'. This removed a mass of committees and sub-committees and a cabinet of portfolio holders ran the council. This was beneficial for the work of the portfolio holders who could develop their understanding of the service for which they were responsible. A possible downside was the effect on councillors who were not in the cabinet. As back benchers they were confined to their work in the locality so some of them missed being part of the wider picture. The move significantly strengthened the hold of the majority political party and enshrined party politics in the county council.

When we returned to Somerset I had become a governor in schools and further education. I had been asked to join the Yeovil College Corporation in 1994 because it had a major financial problem. This was a tertiary college which included a large sixth form. Up to 1993, FE colleges received their budgets from the Local Education Authority (LEA). These budgets were carefully monitored. If a college was in difficulty then the LEA could help out by using budget surpluses from elsewhere. This meant that colleges did not always develop their own budget systems sufficiently well to tackle any major crisis, as LEA help could always be sought. In 1993, there was a significant change. FE colleges were given independence from the LEA and were required to manage their own budgets, which were funded from national finances. By 1994, twenty per cent of colleges were in great financial difficulty. This was yet another example of government making a fundamental change without providing time and support to prepare colleges for financial independence. No family would devolve a share of the housekeeping to an inexperienced teenager but governments seem too often to put hope before prudent preparation.

In Yeovil there was a significant budget deficit and I had been asked to join the corporation (the governing body) to help sort the problem. Some years before, as a deputy chief education officer in Somerset, I had been responsible for the county education budget. I was made vice chair and soon succeeded the chair who had given good service to the college in that role for twenty-two years. By this time the vice principal, Richard Atkins, had become principal of the college. By 1997 we had made the painful decisions that remedied the budget deficit although, like all colleges, we knew that government budgeting also fell behind in terms of providing adequate support for new developments. I was aware that because of the speed of change in education it would be wise to change key roles on the corporation more frequently. We resolved that no chair of the corporation could serve more than four years at a time. This enabled the principal and myself to ensure that there was a successor to take on the chair in 1998. We sounded out possible successors and were delighted to find one. This still left me as a member of the corporation and I was given the role of higher education link governor. This extended my membership to a total of twenty-two years, but I never stood as chair again. The higher education role was accidentally responsible for slightly extending my membership. I expected to retire in May 2016 but was asked to stay on for a higher education review (inspection) and finally fell off the perch voluntarily in December 2016. I continue to be linked as an honorary fellow of the college which involves attending events from time to time without requiring any work.

In later years I also became a governor of our local comprehensive school just after it had been put into special measures after an OFSTED inspection. I arrived at the same time as a new head teacher who helped the school to come out of special measures in a single term and has since led it to consistent further improvement. I still retained my long-term governorship of our village First School where our three children were educated. My wife, Gill, was chair in those early days. She and the governors had dismissed an LEA proposal to close the school. I was the unfortunate senior officer delegated to discuss the matter with them. I am proud of my failure because the school which had been down to thirty pupils, the magic number in Somerset for considering closure, soon bounced back and more than doubled its numbers.

Governors in schools and colleges were always at the receiving end of constant government changes. Each government and each new minister had to show something that would be their legacy within a parliamentary term. The focus would change over time. Comprehensive education, removal of surplus school places, delegation to schools and colleges, a national curriculum, new inspection arrangements, opting out of LEA control, parental choice (really preference), preoccupation with standards in tests and examinations are only some of the political issues that hit the service. Some of the other countries I visited had usually spent time on consulting over complete reforms before producing legislation which embraced all of the main issues for the longer term but our efforts seemed to be focused too often on short sharp shocks. It is surprising that we were able to achieve what we did given the hand-to-mouth rush of the latest political solution to the problems of education. Certainly there were massive problems to be faced but British pragmatism preferred to tackle specific areas without reviewing the knock-on effects of a new strand of policy. As a nation we were always suspicious of grand plans.

in conclusion

---

reflections on an accidental career in education

Our education system is about halfway up the international league table. Our own intractable problem continues to be the gap between our success in higher education and our failure to improve the education and life chances of young people in many disadvantaged communities. It does not have to be like this. The Emmanuel College project in Tyneside proved that well-designed and targeted provision works.

Governments tend to move on to new initiatives failing to learn from earlier successful projects. They are too often diverted by the next political priority. When I arrived in Somerset a senior education officer expressed his frustration saying, 'never run after a bus, a pretty woman or an education initiative. Another one will be along any minute.'

We are not alone. My international work made it clear that no one education service has all the answers. Each nation was hard-wired into its own culture, education history and priorities. In the nineteenth century we learnt from the German pattern of grammar, technical and general secondary schools but in our system in the twentieth century the technical strand was always considered subordinate to our preoccupation with academic subjects.

I began work in education when youth services were seen as essential to the education for life of a generation who were expected to enjoy increased leisure time. There was no clear national plan for education. When I joined, the service was soon to focus on expansion of secondary school places to meet expanding numbers and the increase of comprehensive reorganisations. The emphasis was upon the later Audit Commission's priorities of economy and efficiency. Other structural changes included closure of small primary schools.

In the early years I saw little of the work of politicians at county level. Officers were paid to advise; county councillors were not paid nor were they required to take the advice. Most of the time they did so and education officers had considerable influence on policy developments. Strong political control developed with local government reorganisation in 1973 and with it came the development of corporate management and a shift in the balance of power to the ruling political party.

The focus changed significantly towards devolution; this required increased involvement of parents and delegation of budgets to schools. The training of the head teacher, the growing responsibilities of schools for their own improvement, the development of a national curriculum and the reorganisation of school inspection shifted the focus firmly in the direction of the Audit Commission's third 'E': effectiveness.

Two developments in this period are relevant to the future of the education in our rapidly changing world with its challenges of technological and climate change. Schools now have an inspection framework that is useful for school improvement and the inspection system has the potential to inform nation education policy and initiatives. A good start could be to tackle the inequalities of opportunity for young people in deprived areas.

Previous Publications

Derek Esp and Rene Saran (eds.) *Effective Governors for Effective Schools*, Paul Chapman - Google Scholar (London, 1995).

Derek Esp, 'Employer/employee relationships', in C Eric Spear, (ed.) *Primary Management and Leadership Towards 2000*, (London, 1994)

Derek Esp, *Competencies for School Managers*, Kogan Page (London, 1993)

Brian Fidler, Barry Fugl, Derek Esp (eds.) *The Supply and Recruitment of Teachers*, (London, 1993)

Derek Esp, 'Staff development, local management of schools and governors', in Les Bell and Chris Day (eds.) *Managing the Professional Development of Teachers*, (Buckingham, 1991)

Derek Esp 'Local Financial Management in Education', in R Levacic (ed.) *Financial Management in Education*, (Milton Keynes, 1989)

Derek Esp, 'An International Perspective on Management Education' in Poster and Day (eds.) *Partnership in Education Management*, (London 1988)

Derek Esp, early participation in the following:

N Eskil Stego, Kees Gielen, Ron Glatter and Shirley Hord (eds.) *The Role of the School Leader in School Improvement*, OECD International School Improvement Project, (Brussels, 1987)

'Employer/employee relationships: a chief education officer's viewpoint' in Ian Craig (ed.) *Primary School Management in Action*, (London, 1987)

Derek Esp, 'Preparing for Headship and Senior Management in Schools', in Keith Watson (ed.) *Key Issues in Education: Comparative Perspectives*, (Beckenham, 1985)

Derek Esp, 'Headteacher Training and Selection', in Association of Education Committees, *Learning from Europe*, Longman (Harlow, 1984)

Audit Commission *Obtaining Better Value in Education: aspects of non-teaching costs in schools*, (HMSO) (London, 1984)

Derek Esp, 'The Training and Professional Development of School Leaders in Europe' in *European Journal of Teacher Education* vol.5, nos. 1-2 (1982)